My Other Name Is Mom

Embracing the Realities of Godly Motherhood

Mary Burkholder

My Other Name Is Mom

Copyright ©2019 by Mary Burkholder

All rights reserved. No part of this publication may be used or reproduced in any manner without written permission of the publisher, except in the case of brief quotations in reviews.

All scripture quotations are taken from the King James Version of the Bible.

All sources are recorded for reference purposes only; they are not intended to imply endorsement by the author.

ISBN: 978-1-7334328-0-1

Cover design: Sheila Bauman
Cover photo: Adobe Stock
Interior design: Vivianne Bauman

To order additional copies, contact:
Mary Burkholder
92 Z. C. Rushing Road
Tylertown, MS 39667
myothernameismom@gmail.com

Printed by Carlisle Printing
Printed in the United States of America

For my sisters

Analise Miller, Dora Martin, and Betsy Eby,
wonderful mothers to special little people.

Contents

Foreword vii
1 Created to Nurture 1
2 If You Don't Want Children 7
3 A Case for Babies 13
4 Feminism & Me 21
5 Feminism at Home 27
6 Equality in the Kitchen 33
7 Romance? What's That? 39
8 What About a Social Life? 47
9 What I Deserve 53
10 Children Are Blessings 59
11 Supermom Myth 67
12 When Dreams Collide with Reality 73
13 Mommy Guilt 79
14 Enjoying the Little Years 85
15 Needs of Little Ones 91
16 Our Children's Happiness 99
17 Modeling Christ 105
18 Looking into the Future 111
19 Happy Homemaking 117
    Homemaking Survey 123
    Notes 133
    Acknowledgements 137

Foreword

After one of our terrific southern storms dumped three inches of rain, we had a deep pool of water behind the terrace on our lawn. When that happens, my children always want to play in it. If it's warm enough, I let them.

This morning was cool, so I decided that they should wait until nearer the middle of the day to play in the water. My two small sons slipped out the front door and got wet before I knew it. I was not pleased; they had just added extra clothing to my Monday morning wash piles.

By 11:00, the sun was shining warmly, and I allowed my three youngest to go out and splash. I watched and took a video of their fun, which I shared with my family. "You're a good mom!" my sister replied. Well, thanks! I thought so too.

My boys had to wear pajamas to eat lunch because they were out of clean clothes. They thought it great fun. I didn't mind, being full of good-mom feelings and knowing there was a line full of jeans hanging in the sunshine.

By the time my schoolchildren came home, the pool had shrunk, but they didn't want to be left out of the fun and begged to play in the water too. Since I am a good mom, I had to let them, of course. All three youngest wanted to go back in as well. Since the water was now shallow, I pictured them wading. I figured if they got wet around the edges, they could run around in the sunshine and dry off.

I disappeared into the house to fold laundry and start supper and did not watch the proceedings. When my offspring came to the back door half an hour later, soaked, shivering, and muddy from head to toe, I completely forgot about being a good mom. This was late on a Monday afternoon. I was trying to put away huge stacks of clean laundry and start supper. I did not have time for baths. I did not want to deal with a pile of wet and dirty clothes after doing laundry all day. As if a switch had flipped, I went from feeling like a sweet and benevolent mom to a tired and overworked mom. I regret to say I did not respond very lovingly.

While bathing grubby youngsters and throwing in yet another load of laundry, I pondered where things had gone wrong. Was it the children's fault that my generous patience had run out? What should I have done differently? How could I have faced the shock of my filthy children at the end of a long day without experiencing frustration?

I couldn't rewind. The only thing I could do was apologize. I wondered if that would redeem the day. Would an apology get me back into good-mom status? Was it possible to be a good mom when I didn't feel like one? Or had I now become a failure?

In *My Other Name Is Mom,* I explore what makes us good mothers. My aim in writing, as one young mother to another, is to inspire without setting goals that are impossible to reach. We need aspirations that mesh with the reality of our imperfect lives. Being a good mom does not mean being perfect. A good mom loves God, cares about her children, and does her best. And that's enough.

CHAPTER ONE

Created to Nurture

I love watching little girls play with dolls. Our second daughter was still a baby herself when she held a doll, right side up, to her shoulder and lovingly patted its back. At ten months, *baby* was one of her first words. Our girls spend hours with their dolls: dressing them, feeding them, putting them to sleep. They play house and church and go on make-believe trips, toting their dolls along. There is more going on than having fun. A God-given instinct to nurture is alive in them at a very young age.

Little girls love real babies too, of course. The crowd of diminutive females bobbing at a new mom's elbows may feel a bit overwhelming. I'm sure there are times to say "no" to their insatiable desires to hold our babies, but it's good to remember they are acting on a healthy instinct. God created them to be attracted to babies. Too many grown-up girls have allowed that desire to be swallowed up by selfishness, love of pleasure, and passion for success.

God's plan is for a mother to be the primary caregiver for the children. This happens naturally in a patriarchal system. Dad goes to work; Mom stays home with the children. This only makes sense, since the mother births and nurses the babies. Once, this model was a given in society, but many women now go to work.

The Bible does not give much instruction on mothering; nurturing is something innate within a woman. However, a mother's care is implied several places in the Bible. God's care is compared to the attention of a mother twice in the book of Isaiah. God asks if it is likely that a nursing mother could forget her infant. Even if she possibly could, He says He will never forget His people (Isaiah 49:15). He compares His comfort to a mother's care in Isaiah 66:13. And Paul, in 1 Thessalonians 2:7, tells the Thessalonians that he was as gentle with them as a nursing mother with her child.

A mother's care for her children is always with her in a way that is different from a father's. Thoughts of the children keep popping up in a mother's mind when she is away from them. This is completely normal, but it is a handicap to a woman trying to hold down a career. She may struggle to focus because of all the little worries. Is her son coming down with a cold? Why was her daughter so weepy last evening? Did forgetful Son remember his lunch? The baby seems to be teething; will she be fussy today? And so on.

I chatted with the mail lady one day when she dropped off a package. She was full of concern about her middle-school-aged daughter who had just called to say she was running a low-grade fever. She had to finish her route, but her mind was totally on picking up her sick daughter and heading straight to the drugstore for the elderberry syrup remedy she relies on.

Second-class citizen?
Many of us did not need to make huge, agonizing decisions about leaving a career to stay home with the children. We were taught that it's the right thing to do. But in today's world many moms are working away, at least part-time. They probably were raised with the

concept that women need to work to help support the home. Their desire for children is skewed by the expectations of society.

Since women have moved more or less successfully into the business world, staying home with children has come to be viewed as a "lower" occupation. The modern woman is expected to get a college education and put it to use. By default, those of us who stay at home may be tempted to feel a little embarrassed when we come to the "occupation" blank when filling out a form. We may feel like we're in a lower class if we have no career. What should we write? *Diaper changer? Nose wiper? Lunch fixer?* Everyone knows we don't need a degree to have babies and stay home with them. We don't even need a twelfth-grade education. We may wonder how professional women view us: those doctor's office secretaries and nurses, the well-dressed bank tellers, the high-heeled and mascaraed ladies in public offices everywhere. Should we feel inferior to them?

Simone de Beauvoir, a French feminist of the early 1900s, said, "No woman should be authorized to stay home and raise her children. Women should not have that choice, because if there is such a choice, too many women will make that one."[1] She is belittling the desire to be a homemaker and care for your own children, even making it seem like an option for the lazy. We can feel this attitude reflected in the era in which we live.

Is a stay-at-home mom shirking her responsibility to the world?

Recently, an Australian columnist wrote that she thinks it should be illegal for mothers of school-age children to stay at home. She says, "They're a drain to the economy."[2] It is interesting that obviously there are still some women staying at home. Statistics show that approximately 70% of mothers with children have gone into the workforce, but half these women work part-time, or at least less than their husbands.[3] These people are mothers. They have home responsibilities. Their instinct to nurture in the home is God-given, even if subconscious.

I am reminded of a woman at an assisted living home where our church sometimes sings. She has embarrassed me more than once by harassing me loudly, asking whether I am going to have any more children, insisting "Don't let your husband make you!" Yet the same woman overwhelms my children by wanting to hug and kiss them. I find it ironic that she talks as though children are a nuisance but can't get enough of them.

Let's consider what the stay-at-home-mom is accomplishing for society.

We may not be helping the economy—though that is debatable—but there are more ways to improve society than getting a job. A mother has an important task to give love and security to little ones. Every world leader, famous church leader, renowned scientist, doctor, or author, whether they have done something noble or atrocious, was once a baby in some mother's arms. God's plans begin with babies. His design for families includes a woman who loves her husband and her children and who keeps the home where they live (Titus 2:4, 5). This statement is very politically incorrect, and to a feminist, it sounds degrading and oppressive. But this is not oppression; this is an honor. A feminine, godly homemaker is adored by her family as the heart of her home.

Center of the home

God created Eve because He knew Adam needed companionship. God said, "It is not good that the man should be alone" (Genesis 2:18). Adam must have been so thrilled when he realized he was not alone in the world anymore. Here was someone like, yet intriguingly unlike, him. She complemented him. She completed his world. God said Adam would "cleave" to his wife

(Genesis 2:24). She was not created to be repressed or abused; she was not intended to be a servant or a doormat. She was someone to be adored and cherished. Every wife can be an Eve to her husband.

Our children's need for us is even more obvious. Little ones require a lot of attention and care, and there is so much they need to be taught. Why should they be in the care of anyone besides their very own mother? I drive by two daycare centers when taking my children to school. It makes me sad to see very young children, small enough to be carried, being left behind for the day. I wonder if those mothers mind it? Do they ever cry when leaving them? Or have they gotten used to it? I wonder how many first smiles, first teeth, and first steps the mothers miss out on? I think of all the memories the children make with someone who is being paid to care for them.

Children always prefer to be with their mother. That's only natural. She is the one who provides their care. A mother is an anchor in a child's small world. Have you ever noticed how many books for young children have the theme of looking for Mommy? We have read several stories of a little animal searching for its mother and always, in the end, finding her. My babies and toddlers love these; keeping track of Mom is a central part of their little lives.

Being a stay-at-home-mom is about far more than laundry piles, never-ending appetites, and dirty bathrooms. The children we give our energy to are part of the future. Our efforts with them are our contribution to society. We provide the love and security they need and teach them godly principles so that they spread the gospel wherever they go in life. Of course, we share this responsibility with our husbands, but as we stay at home and they go to work, we carry a large portion of the childcare.

My choice to be a stay-at-home-mom who loves her calling *does* make a difference in the world, and it is not a lazy choice.

I do realize that there are abandoned, divorced, or widowed women who need to leave their children in another's care while they work. The lives we find ourselves living are not always ideal, but God's grace is sufficient.

CHAPTER TWO

If You Don't Want Children

Maybe you're not that excited about having children. You don't feel a biological urge to get busy raising a family. You have other interests you'd like to pursue, or you just want to delay it indefinitely. Are there women who lack the instinct to nurture? Is it okay for a fertile married woman to skip having a family?

Some women do forego having children by personal choice. It is quite possible they will regret it someday.

There are even women who have children and say they wish they didn't. There are books, blogs, and online forum discussions with titles like "I Wish I'd Never Had Kids" and "Does Anyone Else Regret Having Children?" This is tragic. But some women do not have the support of a husband, family, friends, or church family. Too often, women are left alone to raise children. They may not know how to train their children with biblical principles of obedience and may end up experiencing much grief. Such situations could prompt a woman to say she is sorry she had children. There is also the chance that such a woman would be unhappy with her life whether she had children or not. She just pins the blame on her children.

Fulfillment, not feelings

I don't know anyone personally who would go so far as to say they wish they'd never birthed their children. But some of us may be less excited about beginning the mothering journey than others. We have a family because we've been taught it's the right thing to do. And then, once we've had our children, we love them dearly.

Feminists would say that if you aren't overwhelmingly excited about having babies, you shouldn't have any: that's bondage. You need to escape the trap of your home and do what you *want* to do. For a mother who feels overwhelmed, this sounds tempting, even logical. But as Christians, we know we don't get to do whatever we want to do in life. God calls us to deny ourselves (Matthew 16:24). Just as men should work to provide for their families whether they feel like it or not, women need to do their part in the home whether they feel like it or not.

Back before feminism challenged God's plan for the sexes, most families operated this way, Christian or not. Dads knew they had better get out there and bring home the bacon. Moms got busy with the washboard and clothes tub. Women worked hard and often had large families. Today we have washing machines and smaller families—and possibly more time to feel sorry for ourselves. It seems the current generation has become preoccupied with their feelings and making sure they're having a good time.

If we would all go by our feelings and chase after every desire, the world would be in absolute chaos. Sometimes somebody needs to do the dirty work. Dad needs to get out of bed and work all day. Mom needs to get those clothes washed and the meals prepared and a dozen other things on the side. Part of her responsibility is caring for children. The Christian life is not about doing what we want to do; it's about giving and serving and finding fulfillment in doing so.

When your feelings aren't right
Maybe you aren't sure you want to be a mom. Maybe you feel guilty for not being wildly excited about another pregnancy. Maybe you fear labor so much that it swallows any happiness you think you ought to feel. Maybe you look into your newborn's face and feel trapped by your loss of freedom. Are you abnormal?

I suspect that the euphoria of motherhood can be overrated. It is thrilling and fulfilling many times, but it comes at a price. Perhaps you weren't familiar with babies outside of cute pictures. Maybe your motherly friend who loves everyone's children makes it look like more fun than it actually is. Whatever the reason, the reality of motherhood can be an unexpected shock. This probably happens to every mom, to some degree. When we picture having babies, we tend to imagine cuddling them in adorable, sweet-smelling outfits and watching them drift gently off to sleep. Babies are like this. Sometimes. Reality also includes soiling a brand-new outfit five minutes after they're dressed, spitting up over your shoulder and down your back in a public place, and waking you in the middle of the night. Babies are work, and sometimes the joy comes in momentary flashes.

I have found among my friends that some women enjoy caring for babies and children more than others. This is apparent in the fact that some women love to babysit other people's children, as well as their own, while some feel exhausted with just their own. Some are thrilled to be pregnant once again, while others struggle to accept it. This is normal. We're all different.

Accepting motherhood
Being a mom is not about feeling good about it all the time. We may feel like we even hate some parts of it. No one loves stretch marks, labor and delivery, colicky infants, or the whining of a toddler. In fact, the pain of childbearing is part of the curse of sin. After Eve sinned

in the Garden of Eden, God told her she would bear children in sorrow. "Unto the woman he said, I will greatly multiply thy sorrow and thy conception; in sorrow thou shalt bring forth children" (Genesis 3:16). This feels condemning to women: because of sin, we have sorrow in bearing children. It almost feels like being punished for something we didn't do.

We find more on this subject in 1 Timothy 2:14, 15. "And Adam was not deceived, but the woman being deceived was in the transgression. Notwithstanding she shall be saved in childbearing, if they continue in faith and charity and holiness with sobriety." We may feel we are being punished for Eve's sin, yet we have all done a share of our own sinning. We are all vulnerable to the devil's deception. The phrase "she shall be saved" offers a message of hope. Accepting our role of childbearing is part of accepting who we are and embracing God's plan for us. We are saved as we follow His plan and do His will, which most times includes bearing and raising children.

While being a mom isn't something we do for fun, there are many beautiful moments in motherhood. Even the trauma of childbirth fades as a mother holds her new baby. "A woman when she is in travail hath sorrow, because her hour is come: but as soon as she is delivered of the child, she remembereth no more the anguish, for joy that a man is born into the world" (John 16:21).

As life-bearers and nurturers, we have a huge responsibility and privilege. Our children should be loved and wanted as they arrive in our homes. They should never, ever be made to feel they were an "accident," or should have been the other sex, or aren't as cute as previous siblings. God created us to care for children, and He will provide all the love we need. A mom who regularly struggles to love and accept her children needs to evaluate the priorities of her heart.

Mothering children is intended to be part of life for most married women. We need to understand that we serve and sacrifice for God's kingdom. Being a mom may seem far less glamorous than serving in another, more public way, but it is no less valuable in God's eyes.

My Other Name Is Mom

CHAPTER THREE

A Case for Babies

I avoid taking all my children shopping whenever possible, but during one summer vacation I made a quick stop at the grocery store with all five in tow. As we rounded a corner, I noticed a little old lady staring at us.
"Are they all yours?" she asked.
"Yes," I said.
"I only ever had but two, and I lost one already."
"I'm sorry," I said, not knowing what else to say. As we moved on, she stood there in the aisle, hands on her cart handle, and watched us. According to what the feminists say, she should have felt sorry for me, being burdened with a family. Instead, the look of longing on her face haunts me yet.

Far too many women in the world find out too late they would like to have had more children—or any children. They realize too late that feminist rhetoric does not provide the solutions they thought it did.

The ability to bear children is unique to the female body. But feminists say women have the right to "protect" their wombs; in other words, to enjoy sexual activity without accepting the natural result. And if an unplanned conception occurs, women have the right to abort, to destroy tiny humans. This is a tragedy. Women are designed to nurture life, both within and without their bodies.

All the babies nobody had
In the beginning, God blessed Adam and Eve, saying, "Be fruitful, and multiply" (Genesis 1:28). Filling the earth with their posterity was part of the blessing He pronounced on them. God's plan for all people is to replenish the world He made. The word *multiply* certainly gives the idea of increasing the population, not just maintaining it.

From a purely secular point of view, replenishment is necessary for societies to continue. In America today, the birthrate is falling instead of rising as would be normal. In 2016 the fertility rate in the United States reached a record low: 62 births per 1,000 women aged 15-44. [1] With the current rate of immigration, this may not affect the country's economy any time soon, but it is disturbing. Not only have Americans stopped multiplying; they are not even replacing themselves.

Normally the age groups of people in society form a pyramid, with the largest part, the base, being formed by children. This has been reversed. According to the U.S. Census Bureau, people over age 65 are expected to outnumber children five and under by the year 2020. Currently, children and youth ages 18 and younger make up 24% of the United States population.[2] And it's not only in the United States. Reports tell us the birthrate in half the world has dropped below replacement rate.[3] This will bring changes to our entire world structure.

After considering the statistics, it seems obvious why couples should have children. After all, if everyone stopped reproducing, the world as we know it would collapse. Yet many people in this generation are asking that very question: why should I have children?

In some ways, millennials are considered open-minded and generous; but in reality, they are often selfish and narcissistic. Most women born in the millennial generation (approximately 1978-1998) are currently in their prime childbearing years; yet they are the age group having the fewest babies. Why? Because children get in the way of doing what they want to do.

Dangers in delay

Christians too are in danger of losing their vision for families. Some Christian young ladies have told me they didn't want to get married "too soon." They wanted to have time to "do things" first. I have heard similar sentiments, even from older people, suggesting that it is better to go somewhere and "serve" before having a family. This may have its place, but it seems unhealthy to divorce the concept of marriage and children from service. What is nobler and more self-sacrificing than committing yourself to a family and being an asset in your own community and church?

Obviously, girls can't just order up a husband and get married whenever they decide to, but they can say "no" or "I'm not ready," and they are doing it. What else comes in the "wait" package? Such a mindset likely includes not having children "too soon," not wanting "too many," and definitely not having them "too close." We probably consider ourselves far removed from radical feminism, but maybe we find ourselves wanting a little piece of the package.

For years, feminists have been telling women to take advantage of their younger years to advance in the workforce. If they want to have babies, they can do that later. Are Christian young ladies unconsciously responding to that vibe?

Delaying childbearing makes no sense biologically. A woman's body is at optimal fertility in her twenties. I realize if we get married in our early twenties, our fertility seems to stretch unendingly before us. We have not yet outgrown that youthful feeling of vitality and eternal youth. We are awed by the thought of how many babies our bodies could possibly produce. Why hurry to get started? What we don't realize is that we are likely already a third of the way through the fertile season of our lives. A woman's fertility peaks in her mid-twenties and begins to decline after age thirty-five. In our twenties, we are most physically fit and have the most energy, both for handling pregnancy and caring for babies. At this age our bodies recover optimally from pregnancies; even our eggs are in their best condition.

We all tend to view fertility as a right—until proven otherwise. Plenty of couples can testify that not everyone gets babies when they want them. They wish they could have more children, or *any* children. We should view fertility as a gift, not a burden to be dealt with. "[God] maketh the barren woman to keep house, and to be a joyful mother of children" (Psalm 113:9).

Many older women in society who believed the idea that babies bring bondage are now trying to conceive. Though their maternity was resolutely repressed, eventually they become aware of the ticking of their biological clocks. Sometimes it's too late. Infertility clinics are haunted by middle-aged women dishing out thousands of dollars in their quest for pregnancy. Ironically, these are women who may have had abortions or given children up for adoption a few decades earlier. Sometimes the reason for their infertility is scarring by STD's from the free-love movement of their younger years. It had a price tag after all. Now, after enduring the side effects of hormonal birth control all those years, they suffer the side effects of hormonal treatments in hopes of increasing their fertility.[4]

Egg-freezing has become popular in recent years, for those who can afford it. For tens of thousands of dollars, a woman's eggs can be harvested and stored for later use. Some companies, such as Apple and Facebook, offer this as an employee benefit.[5] Many young women happily put eggs on ice, thinking they can have it all now *and* later. But even this is no guarantee of a baby. Many are disappointed. They spend all that money and never get a baby.[6]

Some women do manage to get pregnant at 50, and occasionally later, but I can't imagine starting a family at that age. Extremely delayed childbearing means that women have babies when they are losing energy and may also have the care of elderly parents. By this time, both parents and grandparents are older than ideal for caring for and enjoying young children. Having children while younger means your parents can enjoy your children more; and when they grow feeble and need attention, the children are older, able to care for themselves and even to help you.

We're having a baby!

To all young married women: don't wait for feelings. In most cases, having a baby brings feelings that weren't there before. No matter how much you've been around children and babies, there is nothing like the feeling when you first look into the face of your own newborn. Your baby is such a fascinating compilation of eternal soul and genetics from yourself and the person you love most in the world. Something beautiful happens that I really can't explain.

You know that old-fashioned rhyme: "first comes love, then comes marriage, then comes a baby in a baby carriage"? It's a natural progression. It's more complicated to try to avoid having babies than to have them. Despite the advancements of technology, no method of birth control is totally convenient and/or free from side effects. God keeps reminding us that marriages were intended to produce babies.

There can be a place for some birth control, but God wants us to *want* to have babies. It's important for couples to have honest discussions about this. Choose the right time to talk about why you feel the way you do. One partner should not pressure the other, one way or the other. It is good to allow your husband to take the lead, but don't accept his decisions only to be silently angry. Share your heart with him: whether you feel you ought to be having another one, or whether you're overwhelmed by the thought. Resentment toward each other is unhealthy for your marriage and your children.

Each couple's journey is unique, and their experiences different. We need to seek God's direction and allow Him to direct us. God can lead in unexpected ways.

Benefits of children

Children are an eternal investment. One reason people give for not wanting to have children is because they are expensive. Children do cost money. They cost money before they are born and when they are born, and it doesn't stop till they leave home. But what better thing to spend our money on? We can't put a monetary value on the returns from such an investment. The new house with lavish furnishings and the brand-new vehicle with the latest features immediately begin to depreciate. They could disappear tomorrow in a fire or an accident. The vacation will be over in a short time. Considered in the light of eternity, we spend much of our money on the equivalent of firecrackers—with a bang and a flash, it's gone. Why would we focus on financial gain and temporal assets? Why not pour our resources into an eternal investment? Jesus said, "Suffer the little children to come unto me, and forbid them not: for of such is the kingdom of God" (Mark 10:14).

Children help us to become better people. Jesus also said we must become like little children before we can enter the kingdom of God (Matthew 18:3). Close contact with them teaches us a lot about becoming more Christlike. We learn more about patience and love, and we quickly learn to be responsible, scheduled, and self-disciplined. In many cases, couples with children know how to manage time and money better than their childless counterparts. Despite the "great expense" of children, these people are paying debt faster than childless couples. In fact, they accumulate less debt overall than couples with no children. They have learned self-discipline and responsibility.

Raising children is the ultimate volunteer experience. People like to find fulfillment in what they do. If they fail to find it in their career, they may volunteer for a cause to improve the world. Millennials tend to be do-gooders. They volunteer, they create organizations, they are out to make the world a better place.

Of course, there are more exciting ways to serve: it seems glamorous to travel to another country or do inner-city evangelism. It may seem grander to do something like this than to serve at home. But what could be more important, more stretching, more ultimately fulfilling than serving in the home and training little ones with godly principles? Putting the words *woman* and *serve* in the same sentence raises hackles in our society: feminists want to be served but not to serve. But Jesus said no one is too great to serve in the lowliest of ways—and He said it as He, God, bent to wash His disciples' dusty feet (John 13:14-17).

My children can make the world a better place by expanding God's kingdom. People may say they do not want to have children because the world is in such a bad state. I understand that fear. At times I have wondered why my husband and I brought innocent souls into this mess of a world. But *not* having children is not a solution. We can be godly parents, raising godly children to increase God's kingdom on earth, and counterbalance the evil in the world. With the birthrate so low everywhere, this is the Christian families' opportunity to gain on the world's population and expand the kingdom of God.

My Other Name Is Mom

CHAPTER FOUR

Feminism & Me

What does feminism have to do with us? We're moms of little people; obviously, we're not on the streets of Washington, D.C., swearing into microphones about how women should be equal with men. At least, chances are that's what we think of when we think of feminism: radical women, possibly lesbians, with butch haircuts, who won't let a man hold the door for them; women who have been "liberated" from the traditional home setting and those terrible joy-stealers known as babies.

Though we are probably not hard-core feminists, it is possible we are affected by feminist logic—perhaps more than we realize.

I have long been intrigued by the feminist movement and how it compares with God's plan for women. I feel that every Christian woman should have a basic understanding of how it could influence her. Feminism has changed the social landscape around us; this is not a vague political influence we can ignore. If we are not sure what we believe, we could lose the concept of traditional, biblical values.

What is feminism?
Feminism is a term that has been around for some time, but it may not mean what we think it does. This word is tossed around frequently on the current political scene,

causing Merriam-Webster to choose *feminism* as the word of the year in 2017. Apparently, many other people besides me were looking it up and trying to figure out exactly what it means.

The word was coined by a French philosopher in 1837 to describe the inequality of the sexes that he observed. During the 1800s, British women's activist groups adopted the term. It came into use in the United States in 1910, associated with organizations for women's rights. Currently, feminism is a political, socialist movement that is no longer about women: feminists now say there are more than two sexes and gender is a choice.

Here is a brief overview of feminism throughout history.

Early feminism
Though it was not called *feminism* at the time, the feminist movement began in England in the 19th century—at least that is the first time on record that women campaigned for their rights. Today it is known as the first wave of feminism. This early movement resulted in the Married Woman's Property Act of 1870 and other reforms granting women legal rights.

Things were far different for women then. Under nineteenth-century British law, it seems women were barely recognized as people. They could not be educated and were expected to do nothing besides household chores and childcare. They couldn't go into the public unless accompanied by a servant. [1] They could not own land, and any money they had belonged to their husbands.[2] If a woman's husband died, she could not claim his assets and was thus left at the mercy of charity. When a woman was taken to court, "justice was administered according to a male view of her rights, and of how she ought to behave."[3]

This is hard for us to imagine in an age where women have driver's licenses, shop and travel alone freely, and have their own bank accounts. In the courts of the land, men and women are now recognized equally.

American women took up the cause of feminism around the turn of the century, campaigning for the right to vote—called *women's suffrage*. In 1920, the Nineteenth Amendment gave women voting rights for the first time.

The second wave

Feminism as we know it today began around the time World War II ended in 1945. Women had gone to work and helped to run the country while the men were away at war. Many found they enjoyed it and didn't want to return to the domestic scene. Not surprisingly, home life in America began to undergo changes at this time.

The war also changed what was acceptable for women to wear. The women who had been doing men's work during the war wore pants. About 20 years after the war, it became socially acceptable for women to wear pants at all times.[4] As you might guess, working out of the home, regularly mingling with men, and wearing pants changed the behavior of women.

It is not a coincidence that "The Pill" came on the scene in the 1960s. Childbearing is, of course, a hindrance when working outside the home. The new behavior of women called for the legalization of "The Pill" for unmarried women as well, twelve years later. At last, women were "liberated" to enjoy "free love" and avoid marriage and/or babies if they chose. These changes are known as the sexual revolution.

Divorce became socially acceptable during this time as well. In 1969 Ronald Reagan, governor of California, signed the first no-fault divorce bill (divorce without a reason). Over the next 15 years, most of the other states followed his lead. Divorce rates shot up, more than doubling from 1960 to 1980.[5] This period is referred to as the second wave of feminism.

From what were the ladies really liberated?

Home isn't home

The secure family life that most Americans had known began to erode. Small children spent a lot of time in daycare and no longer received full-time loving care and training at home. The social acceptance of extramarital affairs and the feeling of being unneeded by women damaged the morale of men. They could get what they wanted without family ties. Feeling unneeded, they functioned less as protectors of the home and felt less responsibility for their children. As a result, we now have many children without a dad in their lives. Ironically, as women went out of the home to work, they had hoped their husbands would help more at home. Instead, they strangled male attachment to home life.

Feminists have damaged themselves as well as men and children. In our society, women face a significant risk of being abandoned by their husbands, left with children and, sometimes, without money. The destruction of a moral code and, subsequently, traditional family values has brought insecurity to women that no position or paycheck can replace. Some women who work are now outraged by harassment from men in the workplace—but just what did they expect?

A life of chastity and a monogamous marriage brings peace and confidence to an individual and security to the family. "For this is the will of God, even your sanctification, that ye should abstain from fornication" (1 Thessalonians 4:3). God's moral code is the glue of the family structure and the backbone of society.

Feminism today

The third wave of feminism, since the 1990s, has been a movement to equally include women of all races, as well as lesbians and transgender women. This movement challenges heterosexuality and argues that gender is fluid. Gender is a state of mind.[6] To me, this appears to go against all they've been promoting: if the sex you are born with is meaningless, being a woman doesn't mean anything anymore.

We can see that feminism never had much to do with equality. Judging by what it does, feminism is a movement that seeks superior rights and privileges for women while hiding under the guise of "equality."[7] Women who moved outside their role pushed the men in their lives out of theirs. It seems they trampled over men, family life, and babies to get where they wanted to go; but when they got there, they found there wasn't room for both men and women.

How has it come to this?

A movement begun on the premise of equality seems to have morphed into an ugly fight against societal norms. It has definitely not brought happiness and freedom to women, and it has destroyed American home life. When women lost their bearings on what constituted their fulfillment, they lost their identity, and the whole family lost out. Surely there must be a connection to the high rates of alcoholism, drug addiction and overdoses, depression, suicides, and shootings in our country today.

This may all seem distant if we have been raised in stable Christian families, with a mother at home and parents still on their first marriage. If we have not, we know it is not so very far away. It is in the homes and schools and churches of the communities we live in. The push for women to be better than men and to succeed outside the home is increasingly becoming part of our world.

As modern Christian mothers, we need a strong belief in the importance of our role in the home and acceptance of all that it means for us. We need to be able to pass on the value of family roles to our sons and daughters. They need to see a mom who models Christ-like sacrifice in the home and respects their dad. They need the love of a happy mom who is the beloved center of their home.

We want sons who develop in their masculine role in the church and in society. We want daughters who grow up to stay at home and lovingly care for our grandchildren. But all this could depend on how much we mothers value our role in the family.

CHAPTER FIVE

Feminism at Home

Many radical feminists are women reacting to painful home situations. Girls who grew up in a home where the parents had no idea how to make their marriage work are fighting a system they see as broken. Why should Dad get his way? Why should Mom accept mistreatment? It is never right for men to mistreat women. But two wrongs do not make a right. Feminism tries to correct a problem by creating another one.

God's plan for male and female roles works, and He did not intend it to be unequal. If we go to the Bible, we can see that God believes in equality of the sexes.

Unfortunately, Christians are sometimes accused of misogyny for their belief in the biblical role of women's submission. And unfortunately, the accusation is not always unfounded. Misogyny does sometimes happen in the name of religion. Men may use this teaching as an excuse to repress women and to be selfish and arrogant. This is not biblical. Biblical leadership is a servant-type of leadership. God calls men to love their wives and keep their best interests in mind (Ephesians 5:25; 1 Peter 3:7). We get it wrong when we think of the headship role as "Who gets to be boss?" It is more like "Who takes responsibility for everything?"

Equal from Eden
How do we know God believes in equality of the sexes? In the beginning, God created Eve and said she was *meet,* or suitable, for Adam. God said of this couple, "They shall be one flesh" (Genesis 2:24). This is equality. It is two completely opposite but equal halves that fit together perfectly to make a whole. A man could not become "one flesh" with someone inferior to him.

The story of the adulterous woman in John 4 illustrates that Jesus is an advocate for women's rights. The religious leaders self-righteously dragged in the woman, but though they explained that they caught her in the act, they did not produce the man. Jesus refused to condemn her, instead reminding the men of sin in their own lives. He simply told the woman to "sin no more."

In Galatians 3:28, Paul writes, "There is neither Jew nor Greek, there is neither bond nor free, there is neither male nor female: for ye are all one in Christ Jesus."

There are examples of fair treatment for women in the Old Testament as well. In Numbers 27:1-8, we read the account of sisters with no brothers who requested that the family inheritance pass to them so their father's name would not die out. Moses brought this request before the Lord, who replied, "The daughters of Zelophehad speak right." The law was changed so that the inheritance would pass through daughters when there were no sons.

In Job 42, Job gave his daughters an inheritance along with his sons. It is interesting that he mentions his three daughters by name and not his sons, since sons are typically named in Bible accounts.

In a safe place
Too often the male and female relationship is pictured as a hierarchy: God at the top, man next, and woman on the bottom. This can give the appearance of inequality. I like the illustration of three circles: God the outer circle, man next, and woman in the middle, in the safest spot.

God did not design the woman's role as one with no privileges; rather this is about women being in a protected and secure place where they can operate to their fullest potential. Don't let this make you bristle; there is no offense in this. If we feel like we don't need men for any reason and they are worthless, we are saying God created them for nothing. By letting a man hold the door or carry something heavy for us, we communicate that we value his protection and inspire him to fill his God-given role.

I think it's quite possible that, as Christian women, we have been more influenced by feminism than we realize. The rhetoric that women are the better and the smarter of the sexes can and does infiltrate our homes and churches. It will affect the way we relate to our husbands and raise our sons and daughters.

How can we avoid being caught up in the feminist mindset?

What was he thinking?
We need to embrace the idea that men and women are different. I have been told that male and female differences are overrated, so allow me to explain what I'm *not* talking about. I am not talking about stereotypes in which the sexes must behave in an expected way. You know the stereotypical man: strong, silent, a little socially inept, and incapable of fully expressing himself. Meanwhile, the stereotypical woman emotes freely, talks too much, and turns from her silent husband to her girlfriends for companionship and to discuss the disappointments of marriage. Of course, no one can be neatly placed into stereotypical categories. This is not even fair.

What am I talking about then? Simply acknowledging that men and women live in different bodies.

Not only are they designed differently, but they also have different hormones powering them, causing them to behave and respond in different ways. Even their brains are wired differently.[1] Though we think in the same language and are able to study together academically, men and women perceive the world differently. A couple doesn't have to be married long before one says something and the other interprets it quite differently than what was intended. These differences do not mean one sex is better—they just mean we're different.

Because of our differences, it would make sense to become students of each other. A man and a woman should each realize that the world may look quite different to the other. Their responses are based on what's going on inside them—not on their incompetence. This, of course, is not what happens in our feminist-influenced world. Today, women rule.

Let them be men
There's a controversial term being used by the leftist media currently: *toxic masculinity*. It refers to aggressive and violent behavior in males. While we would agree that it is never manly for a man to behave in such a way, this feminist-invented term is often used to make men look dumb just for being male. In our world today, women get angry at men for seemingly everything: things like sitting with their legs too far apart on a train. Basically, anything women wouldn't do, men should stop doing immediately.

Men are expected to learn how to be romantically accommodating and do everything the woman's way. They are expected to learn to express themselves as women. They are pretty much expected to live their lives apologetically, just for being male. Women's needs are considered more legitimate than men's needs. Women are generally viewed as more spiritual-minded, and they have this vague thing called intuition nobody can mess with.

This is not all "out there." Even as Christian ladies, we can exude the impression that we are always right. Often men seem to believe this and go through life allowing the women in their lives to run them around. Is it possible that sometimes a man labeled as "unstable" or "rebellious" may simply be trying to figure out how to get out of the feministic snare he finds himself in?

A religion of women?

Throughout history, women have tended to be more attracted to church than men.[2] For various reasons it seems women connect more naturally with religion. This fact, coupled with our culture of feminism, has women taking over church: Christianity at large has become a religion of women.

Women tend to project their perceptions and viewpoints into every situation, saying in essence, "I am right. Therefore, you must be wrong." But all that we know and understand is from our feminine perspective. We could be wrong. Men view religion from their own perspective. Their views are not intrinsically wrong. In fact, since Eve was deceived in the Garden of Eden, women are to be under the spiritual guidance of men (Genesis 3:16; 1 Corinthians 14:34; 1 Timothy 2:11-14).

Churches and religious organizations in America tend to operate the way women think they ought to: with lots of love, feeling, and understanding. "Too many men are being made to feel they have to check their masculinity at the door" because some of their natural inclinations are not welcome there.[3] The only remedy for this problem is to get back to a biblical understanding of masculine and feminine roles.[4]

Even if a church does not have women in positions of leadership, it is still possible to be part of a "feminized" church. Women who are quietly in control of their homes control the church by extension. Even if they never get into the pulpit and preach a sermon, no one is quite certain just how much they control because they dominate the men in their lives. Many times, problems in the church can be traced to women. There is no point in feeling smug at the deception of misguided feminists if we aren't filling our roles correctly in our own homes and churches.

What am I thinking?
God made us differently: "male and female created he them" (Genesis 1:27). He made men just fine the first time, and we don't need to remake them (v. 31). But we *are* supposed to help men, right? The Bible says we are to be their "help meet," meaning *suitable* helper (Genesis 2:18). Sometimes we think this means men need to be fixed. We tend to like fixing things. We try to make our men more sensitive, to improve their manners, to make them more spiritual (by our definition), less aggressive, and more gracious--you know, polishing the diamond in the rough. But is it possible we are just trying to make them more like women?

Being a helper has the idea of being a companion and an assistant, not a boss and a teacher. We complete our husbands by being what a woman ought to be and accepting them as they are. Women do change men in positive ways; we've all witnessed a woman's influence on a man's life. But men changed for the better do not become so by lots of nagging. Women who change men positively do it by believing in them. A woman who believes in a man can bring out things nobody dreamed were there. Truly feminine women believe in men as they are.

How much could we change our little part of the world if we changed the way we viewed and related to the men in our lives?

CHAPTER SIX

Equality in the Kitchen

Here you are in the kitchen, wearily washing supper dishes. You know about those crumbs under the table and remember that basket of unfolded laundry to contend with yet tonight. And there he sits in the recliner with his feet propped up. You're thinking, *This is not fair.*

Should he be helping you? In this age of gender equality, where women go to work with men, men are expected to wash dishes and change diapers with the women. The way it works, in theory, is that both go to work, and then both come home and divide the household chores equally. In reality, this arrangement raises some problems.

One author, reflecting on her observation of the movement toward gender equality in the home, admitted it didn't work very well. Some men proudly reported they were doing half the household work, believing it to be true, while their wives insisted they were doing only a small portion. [1] The men did not realize all that they weren't doing.

Most men are not wired for housework. The urge to fix up and clean up is not native to them as it is to a woman. They don't notice everything that needs to be done—and even when they do, they may feel no urge to jump up and do something about it.

Husbands vary a lot in what they are willing to do around the house. Some men will come home from work and make supper, although I'm pretty sure that type are in the minority. Some men help their wives regularly. And some men appear to do nothing to help their wives. This all likely depends on personalities, interests, and how they were raised.

Should he help me more?
Even though we're not going to work, we stay-at-home moms can feel like our husbands should help us more around the house. But before we get angry at our husbands for what they don't help us with, here are a few things to consider.

We fill distinct roles. It's not popular to mention this truth in an age of gender equality, but it is still true. Getting hung up on all the things my husband isn't helping me with is foolish if he is providing the income so I can be a stay-at-home mom. We tend to take that for granted. If we have husbands who go out every day and earn a living, we should value that expression of faithfulness. There are divorced women, forced to work to support themselves, who could help us better understand how privileged we are.

We need to be fair. If I think my husband should help me, but I never have time to help him, it's not going to go well. Deciding who has the most to do is not the goal. If my husband asks me to run an errand for him and I sigh, I can't realistically expect him to be eager to help me with household chores in the evening.

Men don't think like women. This seems obvious. Nevertheless, we sometimes expect that of them, and we are disappointed every time. If our mom, sister, best friend—or almost any woman—walked into our kitchen and saw a pile of dirty dishes, she'd jump in and help. When our husbands walk through the kitchen, they're probably thinking things like *What is draining my truck battery?* or *How could I pay down the mortgage faster?* That pile of dishes may not register as a cry for help as we think it should.

Men view the house as their wife's domain in which they should not interfere. When this idea occurred to me, I took it as a compliment. He thinks I've got everything under control, even if I don't feel that way at all. My husband does not expect me to walk into the shop, pick up a wrench, and help fix the lawnmower, so he is unlikely to walk into the kitchen and start doing my work unasked.

They do a lot of things we don't help them with. It's unfair to expect men to be a second mom and insist they be able to do everything we do. In some situations, I fully expect my husband to take over. When our van overheated on the highway, we did not have any discussion about who was going to look under the hood and decide what to do next. When one of our dogs was seriously injured and needed to be relieved of its suffering, both of us knew quite clearly who would resolve the problem. Ditto for the time water gushed from our bedroom ceiling. I am fine with my husband leaving some "mom jobs" strictly to me.

Men tend to work and rest in a different schedule. A man who drives a truck or sits at a desk all day may come home with more energy than a builder or farmer; but typically, men work hard for long stretches and then take a complete rest. Women work hard too, but we tend to mix a rest and work schedule. We sit down to nurse the baby, read stories to the children, pause to look over the mail, and take breaks to have coffee or nap.

This may have to do with our biology. Men's bodies are designed with more muscle mass and less fat reserves. They conserve energy for the tasks they do. When they have expended that energy, they need a period of recuperation.[2] This ability means they can recover quickly from a late night or an all-nighter, while we are more likely to drag on for a week trying to recuperate after a big trip.

Understanding some differences
So, does all this mean my husband shouldn't help me with household chores? Of course not. It does bring to light some of the issues I may run into when I try to get his help.

First, our husbands generally assume we have everything under control until we tell them otherwise. We tend to think if they really cared, they'd notice we need help. This is unfair. We shouldn't blame them for being callous if we have not plainly spelled out our frustrations. They may have a lot of other things weighing on their minds. Even if they notice we could use some help, they may be afraid to try because we have criticized their methods in the past.

Another problem is that by the time we ask for help, our feelings are probably getting involved and we are not going to ask nicely. If we're upset and feeling ill-used, they won't feel eager to volunteer. If this is an ongoing struggle, don't bring it up at the moment something needs to be done. Wait until you both have a quiet moment and have a calm and rational discussion.

Because of their tendency to work and recover, men do not understand "permanent exhaustion" in women. They are wired not to waste energy. They can't figure out why we live tired all the time. And it's frustrating to them when their help doesn't seem to change anything: their wife is still tired. They don't like that any more than we do. If we are constantly over-tired, we should take the initiative to figure out whether we can change anything. It's okay to admit we just can't do everything.

Maybe we ought to learn how to rest when we need to, as men do. We can get used to living in overdrive. Our bodies are designed with more fat reserves than men's, which provides a more constant supply of energy. We tend to "flutter" more and are less likely to rest in complete stillness for a long period. This is great for keeping us going through difficult times, like when the baby is fussy, or all the children get sick. But we sometimes abuse our ability to keep going. We really may be more tired than our husbands at the end of the day, even though we don't have much physical labor to show for it. One woman's husband said he gets a headache from watching her work. I suspect a lot of men can relate to that. They wish we'd just calm down and relax with them. Maybe they'd even feel more like helping us with dishes if they knew we'd sit down with them afterward.

One thing that can bring exhaustion to a woman is trying to help her husband in business. Some women have successfully helped their husbands start a business, and others help their husbands regularly, but we need to be careful not to take on a burden we are not designed to carry. If a wife extends herself to help her husband and he does not return the help in her domain, it can turn into an unhealthy situation. Keeping house and caring for children is a full-time job, especially when the children are small. A man may not realize the burden his wife carries, and only she can try to explain that to him. Sometimes a wife supports her husband best by focusing on her own role.

Let's not compare our husbands with other ladies' husbands. Whether my husband helps me a lot or whether he doesn't, living in peace at home is much better than stewing in resentment. The man who cooks may not do something else his wife really wishes he would. It is much better to focus on all the things our husbands do for us, rather than what they don't do. And if we'd like help with something, we can politely ask for it.

My Other Name Is Mom

CHAPTER SEVEN

Romance? What's That?

Our homes begin with marriage, but after several little ones, our marriage may feel like it's left in the dust while we race to keep up with the demands of a family. But the marriage is what will be left when the children are grown and gone. It's important not to lose the love in the blur of living. A good marriage doesn't benefit only the parents. When there is commitment and happiness in a marriage, the children find security and identity.

Love and little ones

Marriage is the center of the home, but small children can prevent it from feeling that way. The crying newborn demands immediate attention, no matter what else is happening. Small children can be very "importunate," to quote my husband.

A first-time mom may feel overwhelmed by the helpless new little life that depends so entirely on her for survival. After countless night feedings, *tired* takes on new meaning. Meanwhile, the new dad may feel as though he is losing instead of gaining. His wife, whose world used to revolve around him, is now absorbed in her baby. He may be plagued with his own concerns about increased responsibility and providing financially.

Each one needs more from the other at a time when both have less to give. During this time, a couple may feel as though romance is disappearing from their relationship. Marriage starts feeling more like work than fun.

It's amazing, and at times discouraging, how many changes children bring into a home. Suddenly you don't have all that uninterrupted time in which to talk. You can't sleep in anymore. You put off conversations because little ears are tuned in. And just when you're getting cozy in bed, the baby starts to cry. But it is only selfishness that makes love and children seem incompatible. Children are a result of love, and the beauty of family love is an expansion of the love that started it all.

In the beginning, as new brides, we waited eagerly for our husbands to return from work. The days often seemed to drag. Several children later, it may have become like one of my friends described it: "Oh, hi! You again." How can it possibly be *that* time of day already?

Maybe he wants to tell you something, but the sight of him sends you scurrying to the kitchen—not because you don't want to see him, but because his homecoming reminds you that you've barely started supper. And maybe by bedtime, when the kitchen has finally been cleaned up, the children all bathed and tucked into bed, you're ready to connect with him, but he is now absorbed in something else. He's working at his desk, he's on the phone, or he's reading. You retreat to bed to wait, feeling neglected. And so it goes...

The romance level in every couple's relationship will take a hit when they begin a family. That's normal. But it doesn't mean your love life is over. It means you have to make adjustments. The stresses of children in the home can strengthen your bond and teach you more about being selfless.

Not storybook romance

Allow me to pause here and explain what I'm *not* talking about.

I am not talking about storybook romance, in which your husband comes home with chocolates and kisses you passionately under the rose arbor while your hair tumbles down. The type of romance portrayed in novels is unrealistic and unsustainable and tends to involve women authors creating male characters who talk and act astonishingly like women. A false idea of what romance involves can cause a lot of grief.

True love is simply a lot of being kind to each other. It involves heart-to-heart communication, in which each partner endeavors to understand the other and not merely to be understood. It means learning to care more about your partner's needs and less about your own. Growing into a mature marriage means finding joy in the commitment instead of looking only for excitement. There is a quieter, deeper love in commitment, regardless of feelings, that grows into something more beautiful than newlywed thrills. Sharing a monogamous life through joy and pain binds a couple more deeply than any amount of dates and expensive expressions of love.

We tend to experience more romantic feelings near the beginning of our relationship. After we've been married a few years, the emotional high wears off. It is likely that the "high" of romantic ardor has begun to fade before children appear. The children just test it further. Some people estimate that the honeymoon period for a newlywed couple lasts about two years. I don't know if it's always so, but I think it was true for us. Incidentally, our first child was born a month before our second anniversary. This might be a good reason to start a family sooner rather than later, if possible.

When you find the feelings fading, it may seem like the children are the problem. *The children keep us apart. We need to get away from the children to reconnect.* Some people, even marriage counselors, promote getting away regularly for dates. There is a place for that, but in our experience, it's not a solution. A date night is like the cherry on top of the sundae. Your level of enjoyment is unlikely to exceed your level of connection at home. If a couple feels distant from each other, it will take more than a night out to fix things. A date will likely be disappointing if your relationship is suffering at home. When you're settled in the cozy corner booth, you're going to look up and see the same person you've been struggling to connect with all week.

If I feel depressed about my humdrum marriage, maybe I need a reality check. For one thing, there is no use trying to pretend we're still dating. We're not. We share a life and a bedroom. Now he knows the awful truth that I squeeze the toothpaste tube from a random spot near the top instead of meticulously pressing it up from the bottom, and I know he doesn't close his dresser drawers the whole way. But we wanted to get married, so we should enjoy the privileges of marriage, which include knowing unromantic things about each other.

Also, am I giving, or selfishly waiting on him to do all the giving? A husband who loves his wife is responsive to her cues. If you do nice things for him, even if you don't feel like it, he will likely follow your example. Talk to him. Find out what he wants from the relationship. He may also feel discouraged about the state of the marriage and not know where to begin to fix it.

Keeping love alive

So, we understand the children are not the problem. The children just plant our feet firmly back on unromantic realities. Children are a product of love, and caring for them should bring their parents together, not push them apart. This doesn't happen naturally. Sometimes couples think just having children will bring them together, but it only will as they allow it. Parenting is a team effort. The children should not be Mom's project while Dad hovers uncertainly on the perimeter.

One important thing for us to remember is that, although a newborn's needs must be met immediately, it shouldn't stay that way. Babies are the center of a family's care and concern, but as they grow older, they can learn to wait. They can get on the family's schedule. And they should no longer take priority. It's unhealthy for children to feel they are the center of the universe in the home. Strangely enough, they are more secure knowing they are *not* the center. This doesn't mean neglecting them or being unkind, but they should know Mom and Dad are in authority and have a priority with each other that the children are excluded from.

How does a couple find time for each other in a home full of children? For my husband and me, going to bed at the same time is a good way to catch up with each other. We usually discuss whatever is on our minds before we fall asleep. I would encourage everyone to find time somewhere in the day to talk. Communication matters. If communication is not happening in your marriage, discuss it with your husband. Tell him you need some regular time with his undivided attention.

Maybe your husband is not one who is quick to share. Ask him how his day went and what's on his mind, rather than waiting in vain for him to ask you. As wives, it's easy to focus on our own needs and become frustrated with our husbands for not seeming to know or care what's happening with us. But we can make an effort to find out what's on their minds. We women can tend to think we have the monopoly on feelings. We may imagine our husbands don't want to share or are incapable of sharing, and maybe they don't even care. This is unfair. If we take the initiative, we may be surprised at their ability to share and the closeness that ensues.

Teamwork

Maybe your marriage is not all you envisioned a marriage being. No one's marriage is ideal: marriages are made up of imperfect people. Rather than focusing on the areas in our marriage that disappoint us, we should work to improve what we can in our relationship. Good marriages don't just happen for anyone. They are the result of hard work. Every marriage is going to look a little different, but too many couples are willing to accept a mediocre situation as normal. They would never divorce each other, but they may be "divorced" in the sense that they live separate inner lives.

Every couple once admired each other enough to want to share a lifetime. We vowed to share each other's joys and sorrows. We don't have to wait for a tragedy to strike to show our support. If we would keep vigil beside our husband's hospital bed if he were dying, we should be able to show interest in the "little" troubles of his day.

A healthy, stable marriage doesn't mean endless fun and romance. In fact, for a busy couple with a family and other pressures, it might feel like anything *but* fun and romance most times. True love means sacrificing our own needs. It means caring. It means speaking civilly when it would be easier to be cross and "touchy" and vent our frustrations on each other. Marriage is teamwork. We are in this together, and we should have each other's backs, not be at each other's throats.

If we are to be a successful team, we can't sit around thinking we have the hard end of the deal. Sometimes I feel unappreciated, but I forget my husband may be feeling the same way. He doesn't walk into the kitchen at the end of the day and say, "Thanks for all your hard work today, Dear! I really appreciate the clean clothes in my drawers. Supper smells fabulous. Oh, and thanks for disciplining the children today while I wasn't here." But neither do I turn to him with a cherubic smile and say, "Thanks for working hard so we can pay the mortgage and electric and dentist bills and buy groceries and birthday gifts. I couldn't wait for you to get home. You bring so much security to my life!"

I'm sure expressing more appreciation could be a good thing, but I'm not suggesting we talk this way. I am saying that we need to cultivate appreciation for each other. Our heart's attitude will show.

Children need to know their parents love each other. It is probably the most important need they have. Our happiness makes them happy. Peace between us brings security to the whole family. Children sense the tension between their parents, even if they haven't heard the argument. One of our children is especially sensitive to any bit of friction and glances anxiously into our faces if tension is present. It breaks my heart to think of little children who experience their family torn apart by divorce.

My husband and I are committed to our marriage; we married on the premise that divorce is not an option. But true commitment is more than just staying together; it is proving through the small moments of daily life that we are committed to oneness of heart as well.

Isn't true romance two people who have pledged their lives to each other standing together to face life's challenges? Their shoulders are set to the same load. Their hearts and ears are open to each other's needs. True romance is knowing that even though life is harder and less kind than you expected, you have one person committed to sticking by you through anything.

That's what I got married for, after all.

My Other Name Is Mom

CHAPTER EIGHT

What About a Social Life?

If you enjoyed a full social life as a single person, being tied down with children may seem like cause for depression. A few short years ago, much of your life revolved around time with friends: youth activities, shopping, sleepovers, hours on the phone. Dating your husband-to-be added a new intensity to your social life.

Life may not change drastically as soon as we get married, but change creeps up on us. Almost before we know what's happening, we have several children taking up a lot of our time. Our husbands are busy with work. Our girlfriends have their own families, and likely some of us have moved away from each other. We try to keep in touch, but contact dwindles. We may even have moved away from our mom and sisters.

Bereft of former social activities, we're now stuck with loads of laundry, messes to clean up, and quarrels to settle—activities we don't call recreational. As our families increase, we talk on the phone less; we stay home more. We don't always have the energy for going out anyway. And now that we have a lengthy and legitimate shopping list, we may not have the time or the fortitude for shopping. We weigh the benefits of an outing against the work it will be to take everyone along or make other arrangements for them. We find ourselves turning down opportunities to do things with others because busy toddlers or a fussy baby makes it more stressful than beneficial. At a time when our lives are most intense, and uncertainties about our abilities arise, we are more alone than ever. We may feel discouraged and lonely. We may be wondering, *Is this what I was in such a hurry to grow up for?*

Looking for escape

Some women are so desperate to get out of the house that they load up numerous little people and go away frequently anyway. Some women are quick to use babysitters in an effort to regain freedom. Some women talk on the phone all day, even though Junior cries in their left ear while the other children ransack the next room. Some women escape to the world of social media, constantly checking for messages and updates. Some text their friends all day. Some get depressed and sink into self-pity.

How are we to cope?

Obviously, if we're getting depressed, we need to do something about it. Exhausting ourselves and our children in pursuit of social life isn't worth it. Shoving our children into someone else's lap isn't the answer. Neglecting our children in favor of communicating with others isn't right. Pitying ourselves doesn't help anything.

Life isn't a party

Perhaps we must first conclude that our social life as single women filled a place in our lives it shouldn't have. Perhaps instead of measuring our married lives against a single's lifestyle and finding it inferior, we should realize that our life as a single was the unrealistic one.

In society at large, the millennial generation attempts to hang onto a free-and-easy independent lifestyle. Young adults tend to live at home longer and get married later. Instead of buckling down to real life, they want to party and travel. The Christian millennial needs to develop worthy goals that aren't all about going away to have another fun time. In past generations, women's main connections with the outside world may have been the occasional letter and church on Sunday morning. I assume their mental health was in good shape, unspoiled by cultural expectations of something more intense.

Social realities
Friendships are still essential, but they take second place to the more important relationships of family. Our husbands and children come first, and we must joyfully accept the changes that brings to our social lives.

There are, however, benefits to women friends, and we should cultivate friendships as much as we can. Our husbands, though they do their best to understand, will never know from experience what being a mom is like. Expecting too much empathy places an unfair burden on them. While my husband and I share with each other on a level we don't with anyone else, I find value in sharing with other moms. You know—talking about morning sickness, birthing stories, night feedings, and potty-training. They've been there too. They understand, and they don't get bored with the details. Sometimes we can jump into good conversations with complete strangers because we share the bond of motherhood.

But how do we find time for other relationships? Obviously, we're not going to sleepovers any more or going out for ice cream at ten o'clock at night. Visiting at church or other social events can be good but is usually not the best way to share with someone on a deep level. Getting together in each other's homes is a good way to build meaningful relationships. Instead of wishing someone else would make the first move and gloomily wondering if anyone remembers we're alive, we can reach out to others. We can plan the get-to-together we wish someone else would, as long as we don't make it stressful by planning something too exotic. It is fun to shop with other ladies, though it can be overdone. I look forward to an occasional day spent sewing with a friend or two in one of our homes. I enjoy the matronly activity of attending our church's sewing circle. Even if I only get a dozen knots tied in a comforter because I'm caring for a baby, it's worth going to chat with sisters from church.

Smart choices

Smartphones constitute a pitfall for the modern stay-at-home mom. The counterfeit means of communication they provide can actually make us feel more alone at the end of the day: counterfeit in the sense that nothing can replace real-life interaction. Texting someone randomly all day is less fulfilling than scheduling time for real conversation, either in person or on the phone. I would guess that it is more beneficial to have one heart-to-heart chat with someone per week, or even per month, than to be interacting digitally all day every day.

Texting can work well for a quick question, to make plans, or even as an I'm-thinking-of-you. It can work with people you know well, but it is not a great relational medium. It's not a good way to get to know someone or to carry on deep conversations. It's hard to know exactly how something was meant without the facial expression and tone of voice to accompany the words. It's easy to have misunderstandings and get completely mired trying to straighten things out. Not to mention that it can be easy to say things electronically that you wouldn't say in real life.

And children *really* don't benefit when Mom is glued to her smartphone.[1] Moms manage to wheel their strollers through malls while checking their phones. A mom may sit at the park "watching" her children, with her phone in front of her face most of the time. She doesn't realize she is cheating her children out of the pleasure of having Mom's eyes on them and relating with them in a way that builds relationships.

I've heard that small children experience normal emotional development by looking into other's faces, particularly their mother's. If Mom's eyes are frequently diverted to her phone, this could be a problem. Even the benefits of family mealtime are hindered if Mom and Dad are frequently checking their phones rather than staying engaged in the present. Our children deserve our attention. They should not need to compete with an inanimate object for eye contact.

Relationships at home

Instead of ignoring our children while we pity ourselves for being stuck at home, we can use them to help fill our social needs. My husband is sometimes gone for several days at a time, and I discovered I tend to chat more with the children while he's gone. This has been a positive thing. It is rewarding to talk with them and can become more of a two-way conversation than you expect, especially once they reach school age.

Sometimes we may be discouraged and lonely because we feel disconnected from our busy and distracted husbands. Instead of pouting until they get the signal that something is wrong, we can make an effort to reconnect with them. They may be feeling the distance too. At times we must be mature enough to understand that other pressures are consuming their energies and our need for connection can wait a bit.

Coping with the blues

Finally, how should we deal with depression? I think many women struggle with this on occasion. Depression is not necessarily caused by a need for social interaction but can be exacerbated by it. I find the more I am alone with my own thoughts, the more likely I am to be depressed.

Besides getting out or calling someone on the phone if possible, I find it helps to keep an interesting book handy for reading in spare moments. I don't recommend something "fluffy" that merely provides an escape and makes you feel worse when you come back to reality, but something informative or inspirational that makes you think.

Singing is a good spirit-lifter and can improve the mood of everyone within earshot. I also enjoy listening to sermons and educational podcasts, especially when I have a dull task at hand. Something that stimulates my thinking will transform my train of thought to something profitable. If the children are around or will be in and out, it is better to play something without using earbuds. Someone wearing earbuds seems distant and unavailable. We don't want our children to feel blocked out.

A realistic outlook will help us realize it's not integral to our sanity to have the social freedom we once did. Instead of mourning for what once was, we can learn to find contentment and happiness in what is.

CHAPTER NINE

What I Deserve

As a mom, I work hard. Sometimes I feel unappreciated for all I do. Sometimes I give when it feels like I have nothing left *to* give. Sometimes I want to do something just for me—maybe I just want an hour to myself and a piece of chocolate. Is that asking too much?

Flipping through women's magazines in the OB-GYN waiting room, I get the impression that I deserve some things. The ads portray all manner of things that appear to bring happiness: smiling women on vacation, driving new cars, eating special treats, shopping with girlfriends, getting manicures and massages. The ads send a not-so-subtle message: you're special; you deserve something!

We live in an age of entitlement. For some reason, we think we need rewards, and it's quite acceptable for us to go get them for ourselves. But do we really *deserve* rewards?

Getting focused

When I focus on what I want and think I need, I put an unhealthy emphasis on myself. It's pleasant to imagine I am overworked and underappreciated. But I am not as deserving as I think I am. As a child of God, I do my work for Christ. I live to bring glory to God. Jesus said that when we have done all we are supposed to do, we should say we are "unprofitable servants." We have merely done our duty. We have not *earned* anything (Luke 17:10).

I struggle to understand this reality. Sometimes I lose my focus on doing everything for God. I forget I owe Him everything I've got. Instead, I start feeling like I am owed. If I would focus more on all that God has done for me, I think I would not feel so deserving. I want to grow in my appreciation for God's grace, to serve Him better, and stop looking around for personal rewards.

Dwelling on thoughts of martyrdom and unfulfilled desires makes us unhappy, dissatisfied, and depressed. Real joy is found in service. While it's unrealistic to think we can be thrilled about every minute we spend doing things for our families, our willingness makes a big difference. Getting our minds off ourselves is an emotionally uplifting exercise.

Me time
I've been hearing the term "me time" in recent years: time for myself, to do whatever I want. If anyone deserves "me time," wouldn't it be busy mothers? There are those who insist moms *need* time away from their children. They say if you never have a break, you will break down.

All moms appreciate a little time away from their children at times. Something as simple as a trip to the store alone while my husband is at home is refreshing. One of the highlights of pregnancy has always been my trips to the OB-GYN. Not that I enjoy going there so much, but I like the alone time on the road to think or listen to something adult, and sometimes I get in a bit of shopping by myself. I enjoy afternoons when my older children are in school and my little ones are napping. Even just a time when everyone goes outside and plays nicely gives me a break. A tiny bit of distance refreshes me and makes me glad to be with them again. But is this something we can demand as necessary to our sanity?

God puts our families together; it's not a random evolutionary process in which we end up with children we can't stand to be with. God creates each of us with attention to detail and places us in family groups. He certainly puts us together in such a way that we can enjoy each other's company and get along together. I don't think we should be desperate to get away from our children, certainly not regularly. Nonetheless, caring for children can be exhausting, and it is refreshing for moms to be relieved from that intensity at times.

I was blessed by the perspective of a mom of many, a woman who ought to deserve "me time" if anyone should. She loves time alone as much as anyone else. She too treasures little things, like a trip to the grocery store alone. But she said we can't focus on needing "me time." When we focus on it, we are always dissatisfied and wanting more. It's never enough. When we gratefully accept the breaks that come our way and simply enjoy them, we'll be a lot happier. She also testified to God meeting her needs for moments of alone time when she particularly needed them. I really like the idea of turning this area over to God. He knows our needs better than we do, and He will provide for us. We don't need to stress out trying to get something for ourselves.

The way we raise our children can make them more or less demanding to our emotional state. Teaching them to do things for themselves and to play alone without our constant direction and entertainment makes their care less emotionally draining; doing everything for them and catering to their every whim is exhausting. A mom who is overly protective of her children may feel more desperate for time away from them.

An involved husband makes the load lighter too. If our husbands aren't as involved as we wish, maybe it's our fault for not asking them for help or for rushing ahead of them. We can communicate honestly and allow them to help lighten our load in their own ways.

When the going is tough

"I love being a mom, but it's so *hard*," one of my friends told me. It is hard. The children don't always do what they know they should. Sometimes we feel too tired to keep going. Sometimes the house continues to look like a hurricane passed through, and we find little fulfillment in our tasks. Our unhappiness can cause us to long for the comfort of tangible things.

It's easy to think something physical is going to make me feel better: a cup of coffee or tea, chocolate, music, shopping, reading. Though they can be enjoyable, it is possible to focus on these trivial things instead of reaching out to God. One day when I felt unusually low, I had some time for myself during the children's naptime. My Bible was within arm's length, and I sat beside it and did not pick it up and read it. I thought about reading it and felt guilty that I didn't, but I found other ways to occupy that hour. I did not feel any better when the time was up. In retrospect, I wondered why I didn't just reach for my Bible. I think it is hard to reach out to God because it is a spiritual battle. If I place something comforting ahead of God in my life, it is a form of idolatry.

Idolatry is defined as "the worship of a physical object as a god," or "immoderate devotion or attachment to something." We tend not to think about idols much because we are not in a culture that worships physical images of gods. But anything I look to for comfort ahead of God can become an idol to me. What do I reach for when I feel alone and unhappy?

Happiness is not something we can chase and catch. Tangible things don't fill the empty ache within.

If we lift our longing hearts in prayer and turn our troubled feelings over to God, we can find peace.

Grasping after physical pleasure is essentially trying to make heaven on earth. This is where we are and what we know, and we try to make it what we want it to be. To a certain extent, this is okay. We don't need to live with the bare minimum just because we're on earth, but we do need to understand we will never find complete happiness here. Our desires for comfort are really spiritual longings for heaven and perfect union with God.

When moments of blessing and pleasure come our way, we can enjoy them as gifts from God, "who giveth us richly all things to enjoy" (1 Timothy 6:17). But remember, the real reward is yet to come. If we serve faithfully, we will experience "fulness of joy" and "pleasures for evermore" in God's presence (Psalm 16:11). Today our focus should be on serving and living to bless God.

My Other Name Is Mom

CHAPTER TEN

Children Are Blessings

Blessing: a favor or gift bestowed by God, intended to bring happiness

Children are precious gifts God gives to people. He gives them indiscriminately, to those who love Him and those who do not. He gives them to unmarried people and people who do not want them. He gives them to people who throw them away before they even have a chance to be born. Each tiny being is formed and loved by God.

For thou hast possessed my reins:

thou hast covered me in my mother's womb.

I will praise thee; for I am fearfully and *wonderfully made: marvellous* are *thy works;*

and that *my soul knoweth right well.*

My substance was not hid from thee,

> *when I was made in secret,*
>
> *and curiously wrought in the lowest parts of the earth.*
>
> *Thine eyes did see my substance, yet being unperfect;*
>
> *and in thy book all my members were written,*
>
> *which in continuance were fashioned, when as yet there was none of them.*
>
> *How precious also are thy thoughts unto me, O God!*
>
> *how great is the sum of them!*
> *(Psalm 139: 13-17)*

The psalmist also said, "Children *are* an heritage [gift] of the Lord: *and* the fruit of the womb is his reward" (Psalm 127:3). As I pondered the implications of my children being blessings, I was struck by the thought that I don't need to feel it for it to be true. All children are blessings, whether longed for or unexpected, easy or difficult. Yes. Even before I get on top of a discipline issue, before they sleep all night or get potty-trained. They are blessings. Right now. What I do with the gifts I have received is up to me.

But what if my children don't feel like blessings? Perhaps they aren't bringing me much happiness right now. It's not because I got the wrong children, or had them at the wrong time, or even should not have had them at all. Instead, the problem lies with me.

When I don't feel blessed

Let's consider some reasons our children may not feel like blessings.

Children Are Blessings

We're trying to do too much. I've heard this before: Children are not an interruption of more important work; they *are* the important work. If you're like me, you get that backward too often. When we're busy cooking, cleaning, washing clothes, gardening, canning, sewing, etc., we can temporarily forget that our primary responsibility is to our children. As someone has said, "Too many times the urgent takes priority over the important." When I'm fifteen minutes behind with supper, I'm tempted to ignore that misdemeanor rather than taking time to deal with it. Maybe the green beans must be canned today, or the dress sewed, or the cleaning finished—and our children get little attention besides a few hasty words.

One of my preschoolers went through a spell where he begged me to swing him a lot, usually at inopportune times. One evening as I cooked supper, he asked once again, and I told him I couldn't. "You never do!" he complained. I was about to reprimand him because I certainly do swing him sometimes, but it occurred to me that my frequent *no's* might feel like never to him. He usually asked when I was busy, but then, maybe I was just always busy. If he could have articulated his feelings, perhaps he would have asked, "Well, where is the slot in your day for swinging me?" Do I have time to check my email, browse the catalog that came in the mail, talk on the phone, but no time to swing him? What if I would pick a better time and say, "Hey, want to swing now?"

Many of us have been taught to be thrifty and industrious. But these good qualities can get in the way of being good mothers. We need to decide what we can handle and learn that we *cannot* do everything. I often don't realize until I see it in hindsight that I should have cut something out. I am sure of one thing: I will not look back on the years my children were small and wish I had added more projects. I'm pretty sure I won't even wish I

61

had made more desserts or washed the windows oftener. But I might wish I had pushed them on the swing more or played Memory more often.

We aren't disciplining. Perhaps my child doesn't feel like a blessing because I am not disciplining myself to discipline him properly. Some children are difficult to train. Some seem harder to love. But I will reap blessings from persevering with kind and consistent discipline. Rather than focusing on how a child embarrasses, inconveniences, or frustrates me, I need to focus on what he needs and keep on trying to help him become what I envision for him. Nagging or ignoring issues will fuel resentment between mother and child, but dealing properly with problems brings us closer.

At some moments we feel the blessings more keenly. There's the jubilant moment when I realize a child would have responded quite differently to a situation a year earlier; the heart-soaring moment when the chronic liar hesitates... and tells the truth; the elated disbelief when, after struggling for weeks to get a child to obey promptly, he shocks me by cleaning up the living room "to surprise you, Mom." I savor such moments. There are so many milestones that make it worthwhile.

Their personality frustrates us. Maybe my child doesn't feel like a blessing because his personality clashes with mine or is too much like mine. Maybe he seems to talk too much, act too impulsively, or be unusually irresponsible. Recently I was smitten while studying the word *longsuffering* in the Bible. It means "long and patient endurance of trouble or provocation." God is undoubtedly more longsuffering with us than we deserve. Can we extend even a portion of that to our children? They need to feel loved and accepted as they are before we can make much progress in helping them improve.

We are distracted by other interests. Maybe I don't see my children as blessings because they get in the way of other things I'd like to do. I know what it's like to have many interests that can't be pursued for lack of time and energy. Remembering that motherhood is seasonal can help get things into perspective. There are shorter, more intense times with small babies when we can hardly do anything else. There is the stage of small children and no big ones to help much yet. Eventually our workload lightens as they get old enough to actually help.

Even though it still seems far off, our children will eventually leave home, and we will have more time for other interests. To pity ourselves because we can't do something *right now* is to waste opportunities to enjoy life. We won't have little ones forever. Is it more important to pursue a hobby or to be a good mom now? If we do other projects, we need to know which gets priority and which one can suffer—always the hobby. We can't afford to resent our children because they curtail other things we'd like to do.

We feel suffocated. For those of us who are introverts, one reason children don't always feel like blessings is their overwhelming nearness at all times. They completely invade our physical and emotional space. Most of us understand the desire to just close the bathroom door without someone calling from the other side. Or get a shower, or even just close the bedroom door for ten minutes. Physically, they are in our laps, leaning against us, and hanging on our skirts. They launch themselves at us, tug on our hands, and dig pointy little elbows into us. We love them dearly. It's just that we like to have space. We wouldn't mind going back to the days when everyone respected our invisible personal privacy barrier. Little children don't understand things like that. Besides, they need physical contact.

And there's the emotional aspect as well. It's tough to be consistently reasonable and happy and kind when they're always with us. I am one who rejuvenates in solitude. Since becoming a mom, I have come to love the peace of nighttime. When they're all tucked in and the lights are out, sometimes I listen to the deep stillness and wish I didn't need to sleep it away. Right now, it's summer vacation, and they are all here all day, all needing profitable occupation and needing me. Realizing that they need me more than I need my space helps me.

A practical thing that helps me keep my sanity is a quiet time for all, every afternoon. Those who are too big to nap will read or do something else quietly for at least half an hour. After that, they may go outside or play something reasonably quietly so as not to waken the smaller ones. We have always had this rule, and it provides a time-out that helps us all stay sane. And when I'm really desperate for peace, I admit I have been known to sneak out the back door to sit on the steps and stare into the back yard. From there I can hear when they start yelling, "Mo-om!"

I do think it's healthy to raise children with a little autonomy, rather than being a hovering parent. It's good for them to know how to play alone, even in another room. Keep the doors and your ears open. Learning how to be alone is valuable. Older children should learn to be responsible for younger ones. It's good training for them and gives Mom a break.

Choosing to be blessed

Most of this is in our mindset: if we are looking for the negatives in parenting, we will find them. If we choose to look for the blessings, we may well be amazed. What are a few sleepless nights and a full schedule compared to the adoration little ones show for us? It's so gratifying when the baby stops crying only for Mom. It's thrilling when they first learn to say "Ma-ma" and give kisses. Our hearts melt when they wave from across the lawn or wrap little arms around our necks. We feel special when their eyes light up when they see their birthday cakes and when they laugh with delight at our playdough animals. It's rewarding when the older ones give us small gifts and handmade cards proclaiming us the best-loved persons on earth and when they do things for us without being asked. There is nothing in the world for which we would trade such moments.

There is one blessing of children I have yet to experience: the benefit of having them care for me. This occurred to me recently as I watched my dad and his siblings care for their aging parents as they declined and passed away. In our world of broken homes, it's not always that way. Parents have affairs and divorce each other, sabotaging the welfare of their children in search of self-gratification. These parents become sad and lonely old people without a strong connection to their children. This follows the simple law of sowing and reaping.

If we stop being too busy and distracted, we can have a lot of fun with our children. I love their homemade jokes and unexpected comments: such as, "Mom, this fly is clapping its hands!" Once an older son made me laugh when he said indignantly to a younger one, "Couldn't you yell a little quieter?" There was also the time my small son was crawling into bed for his nap. To his complaint that his side itched, I said absently, "Scratch it." "But I can't scratch and sleep at the same time!" he wailed. And when someone yelled, "Mom, Mommy, MO-OM!" frantically all through the house—and all he wanted to say was "I don't know what to do," I laughed. (Fortunately.)

One day while husking sweet corn, one of my children wondered aloud how long it would take a corn worm to find his way back to the corn patch. The ensuing discussion livened a boring task. We have also had many good times shelling and snapping peas and beans under the pecan tree. The children don't always work willingly, but whether we have a good time is mostly up to me and whether I will stay relaxed and relate engagingly with them or get uptight and nag.

Just for the record, we should not hurt their feelings by laughing *at* them. Some children are extremely sensitive to being laughed at and may need reassurance that laughter was not meant unkindly. Sometimes we need to enjoy them without them knowing it. When they are engaged in imaginary play, it is better to "not notice" what they are doing. We can easily make them feel stupid. We should also use caution when repeating stories about them.

Little things build camaraderie and love. Singing together. Telling stories. Taking the time to play games, make cards, or a simple craft together strengthens our bond. Going to the library is a treat for rainy winter Saturdays or during summer vacation when they're getting bored. I've discovered it's a lot of fun to take them to flea markets and yard sales. Their enthusiastic, treasure-hunt approach is contagious. One of the highlights, when Dad is away for several days, is a trip to the park.

Working together creates symbiotic happiness. My twenty-month-old is in a phase of shoving a chair toward the sink every time she sees me washing dishes. "Wash!" she announces. I usually let her rinse, even though she gets wet in the process. She enjoys my praise for the dishes she manages to plop into the drain rack. One Sunday morning, I didn't let her help because she was dressed for church. She sobbed so heartbrokenly that we were both miserable. It can be hard to let them help when I could do it faster and better myself, but the results are worth it.

The children we have received into our arms and into our homes are gifts from the hand of God. Let's treat them as such and enjoy them as God intended.

CHAPTER ELEVEN

Supermom Myth

You know Supermom: she's that mom who gets it all done, plus a little bit extra. She is calm and well-rested, with every hair in place and no sticky spots on her kitchen floor. She's the lady we all want to be, but fear we're nowhere close to being. She's an amazing lady—superhuman, in fact: so amazing that she doesn't really exist. Even so, many of us are tempted to keep trying to be her.

It comes as no surprise that the term *supermom* became popular in the 1970s, when ladies, fueled by feminist girl-power slogans, were going outside the home to work. Women who wanted to work outside the home had to prove they could do it. Feminism had moved from "we can have it all" to "we can do it all." This created a high-pressure situation for moms that continues to this day, a pressure which I think we all feel to some extent. Women with more relaxed personalities may not struggle with this as keenly, but for those with achiever personalities, the temptation is real.

Women have probably always struggled with feelings of inadequacy and the temptation to overperform, but our society of working mothers has ramped up this pressure. The mothers who seem to do it all put an indefinable pressure on stay-at-home moms. Because if the working mother really *can* do it all, the stay-at-home mom ought to be doing an extra-super job. She definitely ought to be using cloth diapers, making her own sauerkraut, and arranging play dates for her children. Otherwise, she's afraid it looks like she's just sitting around reading and drinking tea.

Performance pressures
This age of easy photography and oversharing fuels our angst. It's so easy to portray only our best moments to others, to snap a photo that makes us look like a great mom and share it with everyone. Social media is bad for this. Moms who spend hours on Facebook or Instagram can quickly begin to feel inferior. The pictures posted don't usually show spills and messes, tears and tantrums, or moms who look exhausted and upset. Naturally, people share cute and fun moments. When a mom who is having a low moment views those pictures, she feels other moms are doing it all better.

The high-maintenance parenting style of our era adds to the pressure. We feel we ought to be doing crafts with our children and designing their lunches to look like adorable animals and constantly taking them to the park. Why? Because everyone else does—or so we think. We can hardly believe that the lady who made her children's sandwiches look like cute frogs yesterday probably shoved hot dogs at them today. Her children likely have pre-lunchtime tears sometimes too, and she too wants to take the fastest route to naptime.

This peer pressure can happen even if we abstain from social media use. Smartphone and email capabilities allow us to bombard each other with photos. Even family photos arriving in the mail can cause anxiety. Everyone looks so cute in their perfectly coordinated outfits, and the mother is smiling so serenely that we are sure she is doing a better job than we are. But behind the photos is a real live family a lot like anyone else's, in which the mom feels inadequate sometimes too.

Supermom Myth

Things are not always as they appear.

I have a tradition of baking cut-out gingerbread cookies with my children at Christmas time. My mom did it with us, and I want to pass on the tradition to my children. So I rate it as an Important Activity each December, an activity worth sacrificing something else for, if necessary. When I look at the pictures afterward, I realize there are a lot of things that don't show. The frosting-daubed smiling faces and adorably decorated cookies make me appear to be a great mom; a creative, energetic, and patient woman. Some years it goes better than others, but the reality is that sometimes in the middle of the project, I wonder why I keep doing it.

I particularly remember the year our fifth was a baby. I got frustrated with the children for snitching dough, using too much flour, and energetically crumpling innocent gingerbread characters. It seemed like they were all continuously saying, "Help me, Mom." I did consecutive laps around the table to assist everyone. The baby crawled around under the table and fussed because she felt left out. And fallen dough bits wadded onto the bottom of my socks and drove me crazy. None of this shows in my pictures.

Being a good mom is not about keeping up an appearance; it's just being who I am. We must be honest with ourselves about our imperfect lives, and especially our limitations. A woman who is trying to be supermom is going to sacrifice something important somewhere because she's trying to do something she literally can't.

Hidden costs

An older mom told me that a mother who appears to always have everything together but is frustrated and uptight with her family will create deep resentment in her family. This supermom nags and fusses all the way to the church, but the moment they arrive, the family is expected to hop out with radiant smiles. This is not a healthy situation.

My Other Name Is Mom

A woman trying to be supermom is tired, lonely, and easily upset. Her children are insecure and anxious, overly worried about their performance. Children don't want a supermom: a regular one is great, thank you. They would rather have a simple homemade cake and a low-key birthday celebration. What little child really wants birthday parties decorated to the nines that turn into a photo shoot? Husbands don't appreciate the abilities of supermom wives either. Her accomplishments can be hard to admire when they come with hidden costs like exhaustion and emotional instability.

Supposedly Supermom Syndrome is becoming a health concern: trying to have it all is destroying women's bodies. The drive to do everything is not backed by boundless energy resources. Our bodies have limits. They can't hold up to constant stress and strain. A woman trying to be supermom is likely to find herself with physical ailments and depression, not to mention just plain exhaustion. It's not a coincidence that so many women are seeking help for thyroid imbalances, adrenal fatigue, insomnia, digestive problems, and more. A life of burnout is not normal. No one should live permanently on the brink of an emotional breakdown. We need to be realistic about our lives and make thoughtful decisions, not go on sheer determination and all that we wish we could do.

It's true that motherhood involves sacrifice and a certain level of physical exhaustion. I want to be realistic with that. We can't expect to protect ourselves so much that we are never tired or anxious. We can't always say "no" to everything in favor of protecting ourselves. At times we are called to sacrifice and give beyond what we feel we can. God can meet our needs in those situations and give us the strength to complete our duties.

The combination of the American lifestyle and church involvements can keep us very busy. It's impossible to withdraw completely from the chaos of an overly busy lifestyle. Most of us can't go live in the woods like hermits, as tempting as that would sometimes be. Someone suggested that this is the struggle of the twenty-first-century American woman. Other women, in different times and places, have faced starvation and war and imprisonment for their faith. The pampered American woman has money, running water, electric appliances, supermarkets—and always one more good thing she could do.

Being real

How do we stop trying to be supermoms? It's easy to see the problem but harder to come up with a checklist for getting off the supermom bandwagon. It will not be a once-and-done thing, but more of an ongoing struggle and a series of choices.

Stop striving for perfection. We can improve, as we open ourselves to improvement, but we won't ever get perfect. We need to get this into our heads.

Be realistic with limitations. This includes accepting help. It also includes learning when to say "no" to outside obligations and interests. Our family and our home, in that order, should always take priority with us. A busy young mother usually doesn't have time for much else. We don't need to apologize for that.

Discern the necessary from the extras. A woman who is trying to be supermom usually ends up doing things that are unnecessary and unimportant. Some things we would otherwise enjoy turn out to cause extra stress because of our family obligations. We can drop the extras: for example, choosing to entertain with a simple dinner on paper plates instead of the four-course-meal on china plates we'd love to serve, or sticking photos into slots in a photo album instead of scrapbooking them.

Slow down and enjoy life. The wannabe supermom rushes from one task to the next, always planning her next move. Life goes by fast enough without us helping to hasten it on by rushing around in a distracted fog. A woman in supermom mode cannot enjoy her children as God intended.

So let's say goodbye to Supermom. She's just a figment of our imaginations anyway: she doesn't live at my house; she doesn't live at yours. We'll be happier if we let her go and get on with enjoying our lives the way God intended.

CHAPTER TWELVE

When Dreams Collide with Reality

We had so many aspirations about motherhood before we had children. Do you remember how their faces were always going to be clean, the house neat, and the meals an inspiration? We were going to be always happy, or at least always fair in our unhappiness. And we thought, subconsciously, that dressing our children in cute outfits would make them behave sweetly.

Fast forward fifteen years or so: we haven't lost our goals. They're still there somewhere in the dusty recesses of our minds. We're just tired, interrupted, and busy. Life happens. It happens a lot. It happens fast. We sit down to supper and see that Junior across the table has something on his cheek. Is it really left from lunch? The high chair tray didn't get wiped after lunch either. Why ever not? I guess I was in a hurry to get the children down for naps. I did read them stories. That must count for something.

There was the day my little son got his shirt buttoned crookedly. I noticed it the moment he came downstairs, but in the rush to get breakfast eaten, school lunches packed, laundry started, and children driven to school, the shirt was forgotten. I did think about it once or twice later, but it didn't seem that important. Late in the afternoon, some strangers stopped in. Before they left, they admired my "beautiful" children. I glanced at my "beautiful" offspring, saw again the crookedly buttoned shirt and suddenly wished I had made it a priority. All I could do was gulp down my pride.

When you're all grown up at last, life isn't as simple as it looked like it would be.

Out of fantasy land

Today I observed my children playing with their LEGO® bricks. They like to set up towns, the inhabitants of which embody themselves. Their grown-up fantasies play out flawlessly in LEGO land. They decide to go on trips or invite people over, and presto, it's done. They choose to adopt a baby or have a wedding. Bingo. No stress involved. This morning they were shuttling their LEGO figures to the moon on top of my china cabinet. At their ages, anything seems possible. Being an adult looks like the ultimate.

I remember that feeling. I thought surely by age thirty-five I would have life figured out and be who I wanted to be. If I could pause my life for a few seconds, back away from it, take a deep breath and start again, maybe I could get in control. Instead, I am hustled along in the rush of life. Some of my babies are already halfway to adulthood.

I did not know being a mom would make me this tired. I didn't know how hard it would be to train children. I did not know how fast the clothes would get dirty and the food would be eaten and the house messed up. I didn't realize a lot of things. I remember as an idealistic young teenager thinking I would never speak unkindly to my children. Twenty years later, sometimes I hear someone in my home saying things in *that* tone of voice.... Is it really me?

As a teenager, a friend of mine often helped her older sister with her young family; she was disturbed by her sister's housekeeping omissions. Now, as a mother of many little ones herself, she wonders how her sister accomplished all that she did do. Perspective makes a difference.

Yes. We like clean houses. We want to serve well-planned, delicious meals. We prefer to have the shirts ironed and the bookshelves dusted. We like cute outfits, buttoned up straight, and regular baths. In fact, these things are more precious than ever. Nobody appreciates the peace of a just-cleaned house like Mom does. Nobody feels more satisfied than Mom when all the grubby little bodies have been scrubbed, the ears cleaned, the nails trimmed, and a silky-clean baby head is tucked under her chin. It's just that it's harder to get it all done than it seems like it ought to be.

One Sunday afternoon, I was visiting with a group of ladies, all older than me. The conversation turned to plants. One lady enthusiastically told the others how her rare something-or-other was finally blooming. The others started talking about their plants too: the one I got from so-and-so, and the one with such-and-such leaves.

I was just listening when one lady said, "Well, let's talk about your plants now."

Puzzled, I thought of my sad assortment of houseplants in various stages of life and death: wilted peace lilies, overgrown spider plants, leggy angel wing begonias, and those something-or-others I never had time to find the name of.

Smiling, my friend said, "I saw one of your pretty purple flowers."

I was even more dumbfounded. I have no purple flowering plants, inside or out, unless she had seen a flowering weed in my flower bed—which was entirely possible, but she hadn't even been to my house recently.

She laughed at my confusion. "I'm talking about your children. Isn't your daughter wearing a purple dress today? They're your flowers right now."

I am grateful to anyone who understands this.

I would hate to be judged by my plants. Why don't I go ahead and dump them? I'm not sure. I just like plants, so I keep watering them occasionally, enough to keep them alive. But they are a dream that has slid to the bottom of my list of priorities, somewhere below the spotless kitchen, dustless bedroom, and uncluttered living room.

Into a reality check

So here we are, dreams intact, but with reality constantly coming between us and our goals. What do we do?

One temptation is to fight back: I *will* make it happen. But I've found that doesn't work well in the long run. My limitations become glaringly apparent when I crash in physical exhaustion and emotional strain. My family does not prefer this kind of mom.

Another temptation is to give up. The thought of all the work to be done is so overwhelming that it can immobilize a woman. She sits in the chair, tired and depressed, so much work to do that she can't do any of it. Occasionally she has spurts where she gets up and at it, but she doesn't maintain a steady pace. Training children is so much harder than she thought back when she verbalized how it ought to be done, so she gives up on that too.

What are we to do when our dreams collide with reality?

First, I do think it's right to have dreams and aspirations. They keep us focused and motivated. It's normal to observe mothers with children before we get to that stage and think about where we'd like to be when we get there. If we have made a lot of critical statements in the past about what our children won't do, that's its own problem. When we arrive and realize that all our goals are not realistic, we need to pause and sort through them. We need to keep the essential things at the top: consistent discipline, obedience training, and of course, always food on the table, preferably healthy, but not gourmet.

Some dreams we may need to modify, like how often the children get bathed or the bed sheets washed. Some nights we will be browning hamburger at five o'clock, hoping desperately that the stirring action will produce a supper inspiration. Most days the house will not look like a magazine picture, but hopefully it will be a happy place.

There may be some things we dreamed of that are completely unrealistic; whatever they are, we need to be humble enough to release them, even if we have made bold statements to others about them. One thing I have learned the hard way is that sometimes I can't do everything myself. I like to be alone in my own domain. I enjoy being able to do my own work, but sometimes when I'm very busy and tired, I can't make it happen.

In reassessing our goals, the most important thing is not to give up. Keeping house is a lot of work. Training children is a lot of work. It just is. Sometimes it takes more time and patience than we counted on. One of my new goals has become endurance. I don't want to lose focus on my goals because of obstacles in the way. I'm still trying to keep in the middle of the road, to avoid both the perfectionistic ditch and the give-up ditch. Reality is here, and though it doesn't look quite like I thought it would, I want to embrace the here-and-now and make it lovely with acceptance. Just because it may be a little different than I expected doesn't mean it can't be a good time in my life.

My Other Name Is Mom

CHAPTER THIRTEEN

Mommy Guilt

Standing before my kitchen stove, I have a moment to ponder my recent interaction with my son. Did I really just say that to him? And in that tone of voice? His smitten look as he turned away has smitten me. He needs to learn responsibility. He has a lot of growing to do in becoming more reliable. But that is no excuse for venting my frustration on him. He's just a little boy who needs to learn responsibility. He requires training and discipline, but not cross words.

Gloomily returning to my simmering spaghetti sauce, I reflect on what a bad mother I am. I mean to do well. But sometimes I don't know if I can keep juggling all these balls. It seems impossible to get it all right all the time. My mind travels far into the future. I wonder how my son will feel about his home and his mother when he is grown. What will he remember? What will he vow will be different in his home? What personal problems will he trace back to his poor tired mother leaning over the hot kitchen stove? Will he even amount to anything? What are the odds with a mother like me?

Have you ever traveled the path of self-recrimination?

It can happen quickly. One minute you're humming a hymn while stirring supper. The next minute Tom and

Sue race through the kitchen. They knock over little Sally, who sets up a howl. You turn around to see what's happening and trip over a forgotten boot. Catching your balance, you notice Johnny hasn't even begun to set the table. In fact, he's not even in the kitchen. All singing is forgotten as you call Johnny in and let him know how frustrated you are. You go from happy mom to angry mom to guilty mom in about thirty seconds.

Not guilty?
I knew about mommy guilt before I knew it was an actual term for a complex that apparently all moms experience on occasion. It's an overwhelming sense of inadequacy. We feel we are not doing it right. We're not doing it enough. We're not doing it at the right time. Sometimes we're not even sure what "it" is anymore.

A cloud of guilt can hang out in the back of our minds, keeping us in doubt as to whether we read enough stories, give enough hugs, cook a healthy enough diet, or discipline enough. At low moments, this guilt mushrooms into a cloud of fog that prevents clear thinking.

Perhaps a child performs below our expectations. We begin to blame ourselves: "I've been too busy; I haven't disciplined this child enough; I should have foreseen this problem." We may even look back into babyhood and feel guilt for things we possibly did wrong: "Maybe I weaned him too soon; maybe I shouldn't have let her cry it out; maybe I should have given him a pacifier; maybe I should have rocked her more." And the list continues. We could destroy our sanity dwelling on maybes that are past.

I did not realize how hard I am on myself until I was listening to an audiobook with my children. The description of the always-sweet-and-fun-even-though-tired-and-stressed mother, who also happened to be a writer, made me feel inadequate. Suddenly I realized how ridiculous it was for me to compare myself to a storybook mother, a woman who was born in someone's imagination. I said, "Self, I am who I am. God gave me children knowing what type of woman I am." It was liberating.

When I'm thinking realistically, I know my children know I love them, for they love me in spite of my failures. Their love is evidenced by notes and hugs and a desire to be with me and talk to me. They are forgiving and accepting. They forgive me better than I forgive me.

So why do I struggle with mommy guilt?

My own sense of imperfection haunts me because I want to give my children a perfect life. I love them fiercely. I want them to have the best life can give them. I am jealous for their general well-being and success. But in the face of my imperfections, I sometimes wonder how they can possibly have secure lives and grow up to be successful.

We all must accept the fact that we aren't perfect. We are going to make mistakes. We all want to be good mothers, and we all want to improve, but perfection isn't the goal. We need to choose not to berate ourselves for past mistakes. After all, we can't move ahead when we're stuck in the past.

Living in guilt renders us incapable of being effective mothers. If we convince ourselves we can't do a good job, we are sure not to. A guilty mom can't discipline well. She feels sorry for her child because she is such a bad mom. In some strange psychological twist, she feels she must make up for her inadequacies by being lenient. When her child misbehaves, it seems she tells herself, "It's my fault you are acting like this, so I must only be kind to you." Ironically, mothers who get caught up in this type of guilt-driven behavior do not win the love and respect of their children.

So many methods

One of the things that can cause mothers distress is all the ways there are to do things. Who had any idea that raising children would be so complicated?

You show up with that first tiny new baby. You're well aware of your inexperience. Then the baby starts to cry, and people so helpfully offer advice: "He's hungry; he's tired; he doesn't like the crowd; you ate something to upset his tummy." This can be nerve-wracking to a new mother. You're ready to believe all of the above because you aren't sure why he's wailing.

I recall being humiliated by an older restaurant waitress who disapprovingly told me my four-week-old firstborn was crying because he didn't have socks on. I figured she ought to know. Maybe. My first baby cried a lot. He cried day and night. In restaurants and at home, with his socks on and with them off.

There's plenty of advice out there. Advocates of sleep training promise you can teach that little baby to sleep all night. The other camp says just get up and nurse them. Some mothers take their babies into bed to nurse them, and other mothers are appalled at the thought. Some mothers believe in pacifiers. Some do not. Some think it's cute when they suck their thumbs. Some can only picture a school-age child with his thumb permanently affixed to his mouth. Some believe that earlier is better when potty-training and diligently take their one-year-old to the bathroom every hour. Others say it's easier to change a few more diapers and wait till their child is three years old.

So, take your pick.

Really.

There isn't a lot of right or wrong to this. Most of it is what you prefer and what works for you. When we get older and have more experience, we can look back and smile at things that puzzled us. It's okay if we don't do everything the way another mother does. Differences in babies may call for different methods as well. One baby may sleep all night with no attempts at training, and another may cry all night no matter what. Some toddlers are going to be ready to potty-train earlier than others.

If you're a new mother and you get unsolicited advice, smile and listen politely. Don't let it send you on a guilt trip. If you want advice, ask someone older whom you know and trust. Respect your husband's preferences, use common sense, and get to know your baby. Babies don't come with instruction manuals, yet they aren't really complicated. Mothers can soon learn what their cries and gestures mean.

Of course, the ideas don't stop with babyhood. There are enough theories for all stages of child-rearing. Psychologists are more than happy to give us more to worry about.

God gives sufficient information on how to raise children in His Word. The Bible doesn't say a lot about child-training, but it provides some necessary direction. We should teach them to obey God (Deuteronomy 6:1-7). Proverbs recommends spanking for disobedience (Proverbs 23:13). In the New Testament, we have Jesus' example of noticing children and treating them with kindness (Matthew 19:13, 14). The Apostle Paul mentions nurturing and admonishing (Ephesians 6:4). Obedience is stressed in Ephesians 6:1 and Colossians 3:20. This really covers all areas of child-training.

In this dilemma of mommy guilt, you are hearing me say we need not take our guilt so seriously; we need to refuse those feelings of inadequacy that steal our peace. But we don't want to stifle our consciences. Sometimes our guilt is legitimate and we need to do something about it. If we have been unjust or unkind, we should make that right. If we keep on making the same mistakes and we know we're wrong, we need to change that. But we should not allow one incident to grow out of proportion as we rehearse all our inadequacies. We are not perfect. As much as we don't want to, we're going to fail some more.

Let's allow mommy guilt to direct, but not control, us. When we feel that cloud of doubt growing, let's evaluate it and respond accordingly. "That was unkind—I need to apologize," not, "I can't believe I just said that; I can't do this; I'm a complete failure; my children are probably headed straight to jail." Beating up on ourselves is never a helpful exercise.

If we check our thoughts to see whether we are thinking realistically, we can know what kind of guilt we're dealing with and how to get rid of it. We are not bad mothers. We are imperfect women, doing our best by the grace of God.

CHAPTER FOURTEEN

Enjoying the Little Years

If I had a dollar for every time an older mom said, "Just enjoy them while they're little," it would be a sum worth having by now. Many an older woman has smiled benevolently upon me and given me this gentle reminder. I have smiled, more or less genuinely depending on the state of my nerves, and secretly wondered what all they meant by that comment.

Yes, I do enjoy my children, but as a busy and tired young mother, hope is the only thing that pulls me through some days. Yes, I understand they will never be this little and cute again. No, it's not that I don't love babies. I'm not wishing away the days of adoring smiles, sticky kisses, and endless chatter. It's not that I long for moody teenagers. It's not even that I want them to hurry into adulthood and out of our home.

It's just that it's not always enjoyable. For example, on a Sunday morning, after a night of too little sleep, when I'm struggling with little ones while my husband is preaching, I kind of hope it's going to get better. At such times, comments like this are not as comforting as they are meant to be. There have been times in my motherhood I felt any change at all would have to be an improvement.

I doubt that I'm alone in experiencing those moments.

There are delightful times: when our friends meet our newborn; when the whole family cheers Baby's first steps; when the first grader proudly reads his first words; when we're handed fistfuls of wildflowers. But much of the time, it's not easy or fun. It's work.

There are days we work with not-yet-shed tears knotting our throats and anxiety nipping at our heels. We wonder if we have a clue what we're doing. We wonder why our training and disciplining don't seem to be bringing results. We wonder what we're missing. We may momentarily wonder if we even care anymore. Some days it feels like we are trying to climb out of a deep well, neck craned backward, trying to see that hole of light at the top. At these times, when older women smile and say, "Just enjoy them while they're little—these are the best years of your life," we wonder wildly if that means it's going to get worse.

Some women do make it sound like their lives get worse; I have heard women talk about the terrors of the teenage years in a way that made me want to go to bed and never get out again, at least until I'm caught up on my sleep. But I have heard other women saying how much they enjoy their teenagers, and I warm to that as a ray of sunshine in a cloudy week. I steadfastly cling to that glimmer of hope.

From bad to worse?
One woman explained it this way: the physical exhaustion changes to emotional exhaustion as you try to discern and relate to your teenager's needs. So perhaps it's not worse; maybe it's just different.

I do wonder if older women remember what it was like to be in my shoes, or if time has kindly obliterated the unpleasant memories. Sometimes I have wished an older woman would come up beside me with a hug and say, "I remember how it was." Or maybe drop in with a casserole and read a few stories to the children. "I think they forget what it's like," a friend stated. To a certain extent, I think too that they do. They're not that kind of tired anymore. And they miss the babies.

I explain it to myself this way: Remember when we were teenagers? It was traumatic and overwhelming at times. We thought if we could make it through, anything would be better. Now, looking back, we remember it was tough, but we don't feel overwhelming sympathy for the teenagers we know. We think, *I survived, and you will too. You're about to find out how much more complicated life can get.* I think maybe it's like that with older moms looking on at us with our young children. It does not minimize the travail of the stage we're in.

One older mom disapproves of the way older women say that to us younger moms. Because of such a comment, she dreaded what lay ahead of her for years, until she got to the stage of older children and found it unquestionably easier—in fact, enjoyable. What she'd like to tell all young moms is this:

> You're in springtime, when it's all planting, hoeing, watering, and continual maintenance. You give constantly, and other than a bit of "early lettuce," there's not much tangible to show for your labor.
>
> But the time will come when you'll go for weeks on end and never be wakened by a child in the middle of the night. Your children will have the flu, and every single one will throw up in the toilet every single time. On Saturday night you will sit in the kitchen and work the crossword in the newspaper while every child takes care of their own shower and washing of hair.
>
> On the day of a big project that's hard to interrupt, you'll get one of the older girls to

make supper, and then appear at the table at the last minute to enjoy food you didn't have to plan, cook, or even think about in advance. You'll be able to go spend a day with your mother, and one of your girls will do all the laundry and put clean sheets on the beds while you're gone.

Instead of reading the same Little Golden book so often you both have it memorized (and the toddler corrects you if you misread a word), your teenage sons will sit in the kitchen and discuss the fascinating book they're reading while you cook supper.

You'll keep a friend's children, and when you change the baby's diaper, it'll feel like a novelty; the 35,000 diapers you've changed will be a memory.

You'll have the flu and spend a miserable day on the sofa, but your older children will see the younger ones off to school, drive the school van, and make supper. You'll sip the tea they bring you while you read a book, and you'll remember how when you used to sit to nurse the baby, all progress stopped until you were up again.

You'll all get into the van to go somewhere, and you won't fasten a single seatbelt but your own. You won't need to take along any drinks, snacks, blankets, or games, and you won't make a single unscheduled potty-stop. No one will ask, "Are we soon there?"

I love her perspective of being a mom of older children.

Examining the nostalgia

Perhaps a woman's experiences with her grown children have something to do with her nostalgia. There are women like the gray-haired cashier who looked at my family thoughtfully and said, "I wish I could make all mine little again." I understood better what she might have been thinking when a grandma explained to me, "When they're little you can put them where you want them. When they're grown, they may make choices you don't like, and you can't do anything about it." I have heard other older women expressing how difficult it is to let go of grown children and watch them make their own choices, especially when they make bad ones.

I think I can see what that's like. They're still your children. They were the babies you got up in the night with countless times. You changed their diapers, spanked their bottoms, and washed their hair. You read their favorite book a hundred times, gulped back tears when they started first grade, and now you've got to let go of them. You have to watch them make their way in the world like any other adults, but they're not "any other adults." They're your babies.

And as they grow up and leave home, there is the very real possibility they will break your heart—not to be deliberately cruel, but because they take their own way. Realizing how hard this must be, I am grateful to my mother for letting go of me as completely she did, and I am belatedly sorry for any pain I caused her.

Middle-aged people have other cares that make their lives more difficult. About the time their children begin to cause them mental anxiety, other cares of life may weigh in more heavily: financial issues, church responsibilities, the care of aging parents. It's a package. And middle-aged moms still have clothes to wash, meals to prepare, and a house to clean. It helps me understand what older moms are thinking when they look at us and say, "Just enjoy these years."

I don't think they mean we're bad moms if we don't love every single minute. It's hard to do that when a child throws up on the way to town after I finally got everybody ready and got on the road. When toddlers grouch all day no matter what I do. When children have problems at school. When the baby who "should" be sleeping all night isn't.

I think that all they're trying to say is, *Don't miss the blessings in this stage because you're longing for the next.* The next stage may be better in some ways, but not in others; it's just going to be different. I'm okay with that. And when we hear someone say, "Just enjoy them while they're little" once again, instead of getting annoyed or anxious, let's just use it as a reminder to live fully in the present, enjoy all the good things in the here and now, and not wish any of it away. Because they *are* going to grow up—and sooner than it feels like they will today.

CHAPTER FIFTEEN

Needs of Little Ones

The day I discovered one of my sons waiting by the road with a handful of stones to throw at passing cars, I wondered where I had failed. Should I have known to instruct my children not to throw stones at cars? Son and I had a talk, in which I asked him if he had any idea what might happen if he did hit a car with a stone. He did not. I graphically imagined a scenario for him, and by the time I had his father paying for the cracked window of an angry motorist, his eyes were as round as ping-pong balls. I realized his crazy idea did not indicate failure on my part, but how very undeveloped his sense of judgment is and how much he needs guidance. That's why he has me.

Another of my young sons plugged the bathroom sink one day, let the water run, and walked away. By the time I discovered the source of the waterfall I was hearing, half our tiny bathroom floor was under water. What was going on in his mind as he walked away from that open faucet? And there was the day I was glad my two youngsters were playing outside so nicely for such a long time, only to discover they were using a paint roller to "paint" the shop floor with waste oil. What were they thinking? Apparently, they were blissfully *not* thinking. At least, not thinking in the way an adult would.

One of my sisters nearly despaired of her two boys one day. They told her they planned to run away. Fine, she said, thinking they were playing one of their pretend games. When she finally located them, they were nearly out of sight down the gravel road that goes by their house. The same day, they walked on the pond "to check the ice" and bathed their kitten in the dog dish in below-freezing temperatures. It is easy to see that neither boys nor kitten would survive long without someone to care for them.

The immaturity of children's brains is scientifically proven.[1] The prefrontal cortex, the part of our brain that controls impulses and planning skills, takes a long time to mature. In fact, most scientists place the age for full maturity somewhere between 18 and 25 years of age. The undeveloped brain is easy to see in the behavior of children. It is difficult for them to think through the results of their actions, and they find it hard to control their impulses. That's why God gives them into the care of parents.

It's somewhat ironic—even though I know they're just children, and I know my job is to train them, I frequently expect them to outperform their capabilities. I am tempted to say things like "You should have known better" or "What were you thinking?" If they really did know all that I sometimes think they should, they would hardly need me. My job is not to make them feel inferior for not understanding something or for being impulsive and irresponsible. My responsibility is to teach, give them boundaries, and discipline with love when needed.

When they are very young
With babies, the greatest need is love. One of my hardest adjustments as a first-time mother was dealing with how needy my baby was. He wanted to be with me, not stowed somewhere while I worked. I would put him down, thinking he should be perfectly happy, and he would soon fuss. But how else can a baby feel love and security unless he is in contact with his mother? Small

babies need to feel their mother's nearness, and when they are old enough to focus on her, they want to be close enough to see her. Probably the cultures where women wear their babies and nurse on demand have it figured out. Young babies are not mad or being bad when they cry. They do not need discipline. For this reason, I am not a fan of letting them "cry it out" and not going to them at night when they cry.

When they get a bit older, it's possible to spoil them, of course. It's essential to teach toddlers obedience. Obedience is a Biblical command for children (Ephesians 6:1; Colossians 3:20.) We can't let them run wild and then suddenly expect them to obey when they're older. We need to help them.

As soon as they are old enough to understand, we can give simple commands and praise them for following instructions. We need to be sure they know what we're asking of them. We don't want to have long, negative sessions in which they get punished a lot. We can just say things like "hand it to me" and "come here" and praise them with a smile. We should never chase after a toddler unless they are about to be run over by a car. They must learn to come when called.

All this takes serious dedication for a period of time, but it will not be this way all their lives. In fact, this intense training time is short compared to all the childhood years. We can't be too busy for this. All that we train into them when they are one and two years old will be so worth it in a few years. Training children is not just for our convenience; they need the security of knowing we will make them obey. If we are not prepared to discipline for disobedience, we should not even give the command.

Small children are like sponges when it comes to things they can learn; it's easy to underestimate their abilities. There are many little chores and errands toddlers and preschoolers love to do. It makes them confident and happy and will eventually begin to save us time. I liked someone's rephrasing of the "Terrible Twos" to the "Teachable Twos."

Training with patience

I have found that being proactive with small children goes a long way toward getting better behavior, especially when we're going to be in an unfamiliar place or situation. Little things like, "Does everyone remember how to behave in the library?" and getting the littlest ones to verbalize the expected behavior will result in the librarian being glad to see us come back, even if an occasional book does get torn. If I remember to say, "Now we're going into the post office, and we might have to stand in line. I want you to be quiet and stand close to me," I usually get good results. My child knows what is expected. He can behave as requested, feel good about himself, and know Mom feels good about him too. It's a happy cycle.

The unhappy cycle happens when I've forgotten to mention what is expected. We're standing in line at the post office and two little ones start playing peek-a-boo around my skirt, giggling loudly. I'm trying to stop them without raising my voice while balancing the baby and a package. It's harder to get control of this situation because they didn't know what to expect, and they can tell they're already doing something wrong. By the time we get out of the post office, nobody is feeling very happy. Too many times, I have assumed my children knew things they really had no way of knowing.

It is, of course, impossible to warn against everything our children are going to think of doing. We usually don't think about telling them not to graffiti the walls with crayons, trim their own bangs, or ride their bikes so close to the van they scratch it. We need to accept that our children will learn the hard way on a few things like this.

It can be challenging to respond graciously, but the way we react is important. Although children need to know they have done something unacceptable, they do not need the emphasis of anger to understand it. In fact, sometimes the milder the response of disapproval, the deeper it sinks. As a child, I remember breaking a serving dish while drying dishes one evening. My mother continued to wash dishes, mildly telling me to just clean it up. I felt terrible about my carelessness, and I think a few tears dripped onto the shards as I swept up the mess. In contrast, making a child feel stupid for their thoughtlessness provokes anger and resentment, and I suspect it clouds their feelings of remorse. Simply understanding that their parents are unhappy with what they've done is enough. This is something I fail in many times.

Guiding the conscience
Children need some direction to help form the conscience. Children are naturally innocent and sweet, but they are prone to act on bad impulses as well as good ones. Just as quickly as a child may lean over, smack a kiss onto my cheek, and say, "I love you," he may slap a sibling and lie about it. A large part of training is teaching them to control their negative impulses. Personalities vary, and some children struggle to learn this more than others, but we should do what we can to help them.

It is hard to believe a child's natural inclination toward dishonesty. I was amazed to encounter the brazenness with which children can lie. Some aren't very convincing, and they get found out easily, but some are surprisingly skilled. I first encountered dishonesty in a classroom, and later, I found it in my home. We can't afford to look the other way. We do our children a huge favor by teaching them to be truthful.

It is possible to mistrust children so much that it's unhealthy. That's not the goal. We just need to realize that there is a real possibility that our children may lie to us. A lie is a natural response when a child gets in a tight spot. The more often they get away with it, the more they are tempted to do it. There will be times we don't catch on, and a child may get away with a lie—we are not God. But when we know something for sure or have a strong suspicion, we should pursue it to its intense and tearful end. I would rather interrogate my five-year-old than have a pastor, police officer, or lawyer do it for me in years to come.

One way to catch a lie is to continue asking questions in different ways about the incident; this often produces a discrepancy somewhere or catches the child off guard. The goal is not to be harsh or to intimidate the child, but simply to get him to admit he has lied and to help him understand that it's wrong.

It is unfair to discipline for things we have not taught. But we will need to punish them sometimes. Children aren't going to do everything we want them to all the time, even when they know full well what they should do. They cannot be trained like well-trained animals which respond identically every time. Children have their own will and desires to deal with. Sometimes their desires win, and they need discipline.

Something I always hear when it comes to discipline is to be consistent. It's surprising how hard it can be to keep my own rules. It's easier to discipline according to my mood and the situation. But children are super-sensitive; they notice omissions and deviations from the family rules, even though they may not say anything about it. Not meting out the discipline I said I would will cause insecurity and make my child carry unnecessary guilt.

What's best for my child

One trap we can get caught in is disciplining our child according to peer pressure. A young, insecure parent can be tempted to correct their child according to how they think someone looking on thinks they should, instead of by what is best for their child at that moment. It's unfair to our children to humiliate them publicly. Sometimes our children will embarrass us. It's just going to happen. It's not right to save face for ourselves with a public show of authority that degrades our child. It's okay if others momentarily think we're delinquent parents. The spankings others know our child receives are *not* a measure of our child-training skill. How our child views the training they receive is vastly more important than how others perceive it.

Training and disciplining children feels like a daunting, discouraging task some days. I cling to the advice given in a sermon preached by an older pastor: "When your children let you down, it doesn't mean you've failed the test. It just means you're not finished yet. Go work at it some more."

My Other Name Is Mom

CHAPTER SIXTEEN
Our Children's Happiness

We all want our children to be happy. We want them to remember their years of childhood with nostalgia. But do we know what constitutes a child's happiness? Is it gifts? Fancy birthday cakes? Candy? Expensive vacations? Sometimes I think it is those things, but as I look back on my own childhood, I am not so sure. I have surprisingly few specific memories of birthday cakes or gifts. What I remember most are family activities. Anything my family did together: shelling peas while laughing together at story CDs, roasting hot dogs in our woods, harvesting a few acres of potatoes, a day trip. I recall fondly simple things we did together; times my parents were relaxed as we talked and laughed together.

Modern psychology is preoccupied with the parent-child relationship. Inevitably, children's development and feelings become the center of attention. This era has been called the century of the child. Is it possible that focusing too much on children's feelings kills their happiness? Being too concerned with their happiness can make us afraid to discipline them as we should. It may make us too afraid of their displeasure to say "no" when we ought to. We may be too concerned with being a fun parent and fear their disapproval, rather than them fearing our disapproval.

It is also possible to overrate the importance of happiness. Constant happiness is not essential to anyone's life. It's unrealistic to think we can *always* feel happy. Our children need to learn how to cope with sadness and disappointment. And as much as we want our children to have good lives, it's impossible for us to always keep them happy. If we constantly cater to them and hand them everything they want, they will grow up feeling entitled to happiness and will find life to be miserable. Their desires should not shape our behavior.

It is also possible to teach them entitlement by being apologetic for not being able to give them everything. To a child, life is what it is. They don't think about what they don't have until someone plants the thought in their mind.

One modern child-rearing method emphasizes playing with your children. I once picked up a book in which an enthusiastic young father recommended giving an hour of individual play time to each child every day. I closed the book in annoyance, wondering what kind of job he had and how few children he planned to have. It recalled to mind advice from a godly older woman who said it is better to allow our children to work with us than to play with them.

There is double value in working together: we're teaching them to work and building relationships at the same time. I learn the most about what's going on with my older children when I am working with one of them. When their hands are busy drying dishes, I hear a lot about school and other things that are on their minds.

There is definitely a place for families to do activities together. Our family enjoys cozy winter evenings with various board games spread out on the living room floor. Sometimes my husband or I may draw or paint with the children or do some other project. Sometimes we may surprise our little ones by briefly entering their play world and giving them some new ideas, but we have not found it necessary to their happiness to crawl around on the floor pushing a truck for an hour. We are their parents after all, not their buddies.

Childhood in the past

Times have changed in the last one hundred years or so. During the Industrial Revolution, many children worked to help support their families. Children had always worked at home on the farm, but with the beginning of mass production, poor families moved into the city and sent their children to work in factories.[1] Children as young as six worked long hours in dangerous conditions, doing adult's work. It is obvious these children stopped playing at a much younger age than children of today.

These little employees, working long hours in dangerous conditions, had their childhood stolen from them. I can't imagine my ten-year-old son going to work in a coal mine for twelve hours a day, or my eight-year-old daughter standing on a stool winding thread onto bobbins for ten hours a day. Photographs of child laborers during this time depict sad and exhausted-looking children.[2] Child labor laws were a necessary thing. But it seems the pendulum has swung wildly in the other direction.

I struggle to keep my children profitably occupied during summer vacation. I can only come up with so many age-appropriate tasks. And sometimes they become bored with ample play time, even though they have blocks, matchbox cars, LEGOs, books, and dolls enough to supply a small daycare. This is not the only thing that has changed. In bygone days, children were taught to be seen and not heard. Remember Almanzo in *Farmer Boy*? This sounds quite strict to us, but perhaps we have relaxed too much. Somehow, we have gotten to where it's okay for very young children to participate in, and at times even dominate, adult conversation.

Is it possible that modern children's feelings are catered to in a way that is unhealthy? Children need to grow up knowing they are children, not extra-clever miniature adults. They do not develop a healthy respect for authority when they are treated as equals. I am not advocating being unkind to our children, simply relating to them as one who has authority over them.

What makes children happy?
The ultrasound technician at my OB-GYN office, a pleasant older woman, was curious about the Mennonites. "Do you keep your young people?" she wondered. She confided her disappointment in her grown daughter who had dropped out of college and was living at home doing drugs.

My husband and I know a few other older folks in our area of the South who are bewildered as to why their delinquent adult children are coping with life by using drugs. They don't know what went wrong. We wonder if it could be caused, in part, by departing from the old methods of "tail beatin'," to quote our southern neighbor. (I do not believe in beating children. This refers to a deliberate spanking on the proper portion of the anatomy.)

As a teenager, I babysat a precocious neighbor boy part-time, son of a professor mother and a stay-at-home dad. He had been taught to read at the age of three. His parent's world revolved around him. Suspecting that my parents were of the old-fashioned school of spanking, they requested that their son should never witness a spanking of my younger siblings. (I guess they didn't know spankings were private affairs.) His parents seemed determined to keep him perfectly happy and never rock his boat, but he was a stubborn and irritable child. I have often wondered what has become of him. His parents seemed to expect him to be the next Einstein. But lack of parental discipline results in a lack of the self-discipline that gives a child the necessary basis for succeeding in life.

In an informal survey, I asked fifteen adults what made their childhood happy. The things they *didn't* mention were thought-provoking. They didn't say things my children sometimes beg for, things they think will make them happy. Missing from the list were bubble gum, RipStiks, LEGOs, porcelain dolls, and roller skates. I suddenly wondered why we buy our children gifts. I realize the gesture is meaningful, apart from the actual gift. But probably every parent knows the frustration of finally spending money on a long-coveted item, seeing it played with intensely for three days, and then finding it has disappeared into the back of the closet for the next six weeks or was donated to a sibling because "I'm tired of playing with it." And bubblegum? I did not know a child could chew sixteen pieces in two days and expect to get more next time we're in town. Children don't know what brings them happiness.

Here are the results of my little childhood-happiness survey.

Doing things as a family topped the list. Seven mentioned this, including details of activities such as playing games, camping, cookouts, baking cookies, or reading together on cozy winter evenings.

Closely related to that, five mentioned working with a parent or riding along with Dad.

Four people said that knowing their parents or other adults cared about them made them happy.

Three mentioned playing outside with siblings.

Three people said it was having books to read.

Two people fondly remembered playing with pets.

One recalled a doll's tea party attended by her mother.

One said her grandma was part of her happiest memories.

One mentioned family worship.

One said it was feeling his parents' approval.

And my favorite: "I think I was happy when my parents were happy."

What I take from this is that the average child with ordinary, well-intentioned parents is happy.

Throw in a board game, a few cookouts, some books, a backyard, and maybe a pet, and we have a simple recipe for happiness that costs very little.

Happiness protected
On the dark side, conducting the survey reminded me that some people must think harder to remember happy times. Abusive situations mar the happiness. Molestation can happen to children with good parents. It can happen right in the home. We cannot overestimate the value of knowing what is going on if our children are to grow up feeling that we care. Children need to feel safe.

It is physically impossible for a mother to keep her eyes on all her children one hundred percent of their first eighteen years, but this is not a cause for despair or anxiety. There are ways to protect our children: teaching them appropriate behavior, knowing where they are and who they are with, not allowing them to be with others behind closed doors or unsupervised on another level of the house. We can't afford to be naïve: a teen or adult with an unusual interest in our child may not be a role model at all. We can be alert for changes in their demeanor and try to have such a good relationship with them that they are not afraid to talk to us. This is not to say nothing could ever happen to our children, but we can do our best to prevent abuse so extensive that our children grow up feeling we didn't care about them.

Am I responsible for my child's overall happiness? Yes. But not in the sense that happiness is the goal. True happiness will mean momentary sadness sometimes. It is a byproduct of other things. It means I will sometimes say "no" to something they want. It means discipline. It means they must learn to do things they don't like to do and learn not to do things they might like to do. It means they must learn life is not all about them. And the sooner they learn it, the happier they will be.

CHAPTER SEVENTEEN

Modeling Christ

You've heard these maxims: "More is caught than taught" and "What you are speaks so loudly I can't hear what you're saying." Recently I heard something like this: "Despite their best efforts to train them differently, children continue to have their parent's bad manners." Our talk and teaching are mostly ineffective if our children do not see us modeling the standard we hold out to them. This is frightening, because I am far from what I wish to be.

A living example

It is impossible to boost our children to a level we are unwilling to climb to ourselves. Children observe, they sense who we really are, and they pattern themselves after what they see. One-and two-year-olds make us smile by copying words and actions they don't even understand. Older children don't stop doing that. The ancient proverb is still true: "As is the mother, so is her daughter" (Ezekiel 16:44). How can we reconcile the reality of our failures with the fact that we are trying to teach our children to live righteously? We have to be real with ourselves. If the way I live implies that it's okay for me but not for them, they will soon view me as a hypocrite.

It is good for me to teach my children God's ways. It is good for them to hear me pray and see me reading my Bible, but it is even better for them to see me respond in a Christ-like way to a provoking situation. Abstract Christianity is easy; making theology real in my life is more difficult. I must be a doer of Jesus' ways; not just a hearer of them. Jesus taught a lot about our actions. He said people are known by their "fruits," the products of their lives.

Living a double life of saying one thing and doing another will confuse and repel our children. In 2 Timothy, Paul commends Timothy for his "unfeigned faith" which "dwelt first" in his grandmother, then in his mother, and now in him. *Unfeigned* means sincere or genuine. This is encouraging; none of us can be perfect, but we can be sincere.

Growing pains
I was a better Christian before I was a mother. At least it seems like I was. I read my Bible more. I took notes from sermons. I didn't get upset as often. I seldom said things I regretted. When life was easier, it was easier to be good. But was I really a better Christian?

If I had more time to read my Bible, was I better than I am when rushing around trying to pack lunches, start laundry, make breakfast, and take the children to school? If I had two free hands to take notes, was I better than I am when pacing the hall with a fussy baby hoping the sermon is short, or nodding off in a nursery rocker? If I didn't feel frustrated because I wasn't overwhelmed, exhausted, and pulled in five directions, was I really "keeping my temper"? Thankfully, I don't need to decide this.

God knows my desire to be faithful. It does seem that motherhood has made the difficulty of living the Christian life become a reality for me. I think I only now begin to see what it's all about, to see who I really am and Who God really is. When I fail and fall flat on my face, my own inadequacy becomes clearer, and I grow in understanding God's patience and love toward me. Through the ups and downs of life with children, I think I may become someone I could not have otherwise.

In the low moments

Being a mother has a way of showing up the worst in us. It is not something we can study for; then ace all the tests. Nothing can prepare you for caring for children twenty-four hours a day, seven days a week. I was the oldest of nine children. I babysat as a teenager. I taught many Sunday school and summer Bible school classes. I taught school for two years and, after that, did substitute teaching. I enjoyed working with children, and I thought I knew a fair amount about relating to them. It was all valuable experience, but it isn't enough to prevent me from getting upset when I have a tired headache and my children are being wild, ridiculous, or disobedient—or all three at once. I can completely relate to the teacher-turned mother who said, "I didn't know I had a temper until I had children."

Our children can bring out profound feelings of tenderness in us, but they are not always sweet and cute. Sometimes they are naughty and annoying. Even though we would be devastated were we to lose a child, there may be times they awaken raw anger in us.

I observed a mother become increasingly frustrated with her daughter who obviously had not been trained to obey well but was old enough to know better. I could feel the mother's blood pressure rising, just by watching her clenched jaw and angry glare as her daughter refused to obey. When she walked by me, she said, "I need God to gimme some patience!"

Yes. Me too! It sure would be nice if He would hand it out. "I need a piece of patience to get me through the day, God. Please make it a big piece." But it doesn't work that way. In fact, sometimes God seems silent and far away during an emotional crisis. Rather than making it easy for us, He allows more trials to help us develop patience (James 1:3).

Survival tips

Take responsibility for your physical and emotional well-being. A primary reason mothers become short-fused is because they are tired. We should try to avoid taking on big projects during especially sleep-deprived seasons. When we have a newborn, our lives usually can't stretch to include much more than the baby, especially if we have other children. Sometimes we may need to ask for help. If we find ourselves in a situation we can't change—for example, the baby screams night after night and life must go on—God will be there. One practical way God provides for a busy young mother is with lactation-induced hormones that help keep us relaxed. God intends for us to be mothers, and He will provide for us.

Deal with your own issues. Frustration with our children can be a sign of turbulence within. Something nagging at us that we aren't dealing with can spill out on our innocent and unsuspecting children. I have found that often when I feel cross with the children, I am actually upset about something else. It may be something I am worried about or something I need to talk with someone about.

Living with the uncannily sharp eyes and brains of little people places us under intense and constant scrutiny. I can't hide who I really am. My secret fears, hidden sins, and unresolved insecurities are likely to manifest themselves in my children, not because of a generational curse or spiritual oppression, but because they can sense what really resides in my heart. We are all broken and imperfect in some way. The key is to be on the road toward wholeness, not to pretend we're not broken.

Admit your imperfections. This is one of the keys to being genuine. We aren't perfect. Our children know that. Pretending we don't make mistakes isn't going to fool them. We get upset; we react to their foolish ways ungraciously; we say things we regret. The only way we can live sincerely before them is to apologize when we have done wrong. No matter how little, they deserve an "I'm sorry" sometimes.

Honor your husband. Older, wiser people often link the health of the marriage relationship to the children's spiritual success. Children need to know that Dad loves Mom and that Mom respects Dad. Oddly enough, when a woman respects her husband, she tends to win respect from her children. A woman living in defiance of her husband and other authorities in her life will struggle to get respect from her children.

Part of honoring our husbands is sharing goals for our children. Doing our own thing with the children without his support is unlikely to be successful. We won't always agree exactly on how to train and discipline the children, but all disagreements should take place in private. We should discuss our children's problems with our husbands before going to others. Asking others' advice is best done with our husband's knowledge and consent.

Endure to the end. There is no magic key that opens the door to victory; we have to buckle down and endure. We need to keep picking ourselves up and trying again. In this way, we press on toward perfection (James 1:4). We grow in patience as we learn to exercise self-restraint (2 Peter 1:6), and we become fruitful in Christ (2 Peter 1:8).

Sharing our faith

Finally, let's not be shy about letting our children see our faith. We don't need to share everything that's in our hearts, but neither should we keep it all hidden. It has been meaningful to me to get glimpses into my mother's spiritual journey. I know she gets up early to pray for her children. I know some of her favorite Bible verses and at least one of her favorite hymns. I can still quote an inspirational poem she had taped to the inside of a cupboard door when I was a teenager.

Our faith may seem weak and inadequate many times, but God can work in us best when we know how much we need Him. Let's open our hearts to His leading and live humbly and honestly before our children.

CHAPTER EIGHTEEN

Looking into the Future

Sometimes I worry about my children. I can't help it. I worry about their health, their grades, and their behavior. I worry about their future: what they will become, who they will marry.

I read somewhere that a mom can only be as happy as her least happy child. I didn't know when they were born that my sweet, helpless babies would affect my happiness so profoundly. I didn't know they would always be in my heart. I didn't understand that their sadness would be my sorrow, their bad behavior my grief. I did not know the potential for worry.

Sometimes, overwhelmed by the condition of the world and the impending loss of my children's innocence, I wish I could keep them young and safe inside the walls of my home. But I know they must grow up and go away from my care; they will make their own choices in a world where there are a lot of bad options.

I realize acutely that despite my best efforts, my children must make a personal choice whether to live for Christ or self—and they really might not choose Christ. Some would say that if you do everything right, your children are guaranteed to turn out well. Only people whose children are all grown and reasonably meeting their parents' expectations can say that with confidence.

I attempt to turn my children toward Christ and away from sin. The choice will ultimately be theirs.

"Sometimes I wonder whether all of my children will turn out well," I confided to a friend.

"Sometimes I wonder whether *any* of mine will turn out well!" she responded.

Being a mom is like that.

I asked an older mom what advice she would have given to her younger self. Her words reassured me: "*Relax!* I worried too much that they weren't going to turn out." Her next comment was humbling as well as comforting. "Our children forgive so much in us."

Sometimes I observe families with older children, trying to analyze their secret to success. Were they strict? Were they lenient? I've almost given up on that. The best of homes seems always to have at least one fairly major flaw, and the worst domestic situations have turned out some of the sweetest people. So, I conclude that there is no magic formula to guarantee success. I live my life to the best of my abilities, and the results rest in the grace of God.

This doesn't mean I should just sit on my hands and hope for the best. I should do all that I can to help my children. But what can I do?

Too busy to care?

Observing conservative Christians, one person commented, "They love children, but they don't act like they love them." This is disturbing. It seems it may be difficult to have a good work ethic and meet the emotional needs of our children at the same time. Children can be well-clothed, fed, educated—provided for in every way—and yet feel their parents have no time for them. It has been said that if parents want their children to turn out well, they should spend half as much money on them and twice as much time.

It frustrates me how the very things we do for our families become their enemies. I cook, clean, garden, sew, wash the clothes. Caught on the treadmill of duty, I rush past my family. The things I do to meet the physical needs of my children can keep me from spending time with them and make me tired and anxious. I become my own "exacting mistress," as one husband called his wife when she was exerting herself too much over home duties, becoming anxious and irritable.[1] I have yet to find a simple solution to this dilemma, but I hope an awareness of the conflict helps me make more conscientious decisions.

One week recently, caught up in the summer frenzy of pickle preserving, tomato juicing, and green been canning, I was discouraged by the general grouchiness and bickering among my children. In hindsight, I realized their behavior was probably a barometer, warning me that our schedule was too hectic.

Sometimes on the busiest mornings, the littlest ones follow me around and cry or grump about everything. But if I just drop everything and sit down and read to them, it usually solves the problem. A few minutes of my attention can do wonders. Soon they run off to play, and I can get back to work.

One of the things that can keep us from being aware of our children's emotional needs is being with them so much. I am well aware they are in my home. I say, "You forgot to make your bed. Pick up your dirty socks. Don't talk with your mouth full." But I can give those orders without even making eye contact. In the bustle of things to do, I might not notice someone's countenance is troubled when they come home from school. I might not pick up on odd behavior stemming from an event they'd like to talk about. I might just scold when the "acting out" is a cry for attention. My children do not need to be smothered and catered to, but they do need me to pay attention to them and make them feel wanted in my home. They need to know I'm listening when they talk about problems that seem small to me but large to them. They need to know I care when someone was unkind or something was disappointing. Sometimes they need me to personally put the Band-aid on, because it's about more than the Band-aid.

One mother of older children said you must care about their "little" troubles when they are small if you want a close relationship with them as teenagers. Their problems are real and distressing to them; if they get the feeling we don't care, it will be hard to convince them we care about their problems when they get older.

Emotional needs
Children's needs vary. Some need touch; they are always cozying up to me. Some need my time; they want me to look at something or do something with them. Some show their desire for little gifts and notes by showering them on me. As children grow older, their love languages usually become more apparent, and we can use that to our advantage.

Thinking of the needs of our children can be overwhelming, especially for mothers of large families. It's easy to worry that someone is falling through the cracks. I look at mothers who have teenagers and babies at the same time and wonder how they do it. One such mother told me she wished someone would tell her how to meet all her children's needs. All I can say is that if your heart is toward your children, they will feel that. God's grace is always sufficient. If He loves for women to bear children, surely He loves to help them meet the needs of those children.

One mother of both older and younger children related a practical way she met her children's needs at a stressful time in her life. Her husband is a busy ordained man. At one point she was caring for her sick mother, helping a married daughter through a crisis, and planning a wedding for another daughter. She sat down with her children and told them she was concerned they would feel she was neglecting them, and she didn't want that to happen. She assured them she cared and asked them to please let her know if they wanted to talk about something. Over the next few days, one by one they came and said, "Mom, can we talk?" She had communicated that she cared even though her life was hectic.

Finally, let's always pray for our children. We should never underestimate the power of prayer. We've all heard stories about the influence of a praying mother, and I am thankful to be the daughter of a praying mother.

Raising children is the biggest, scariest, loveliest, and possibly the most painful thing I will ever undertake, but worrying about the future helps nothing. Jesus said, "Take therefore no thought for the morrow: for the morrow shall take thought for the things of itself" (Matthew 6:34). We can't see the end of the journey, but we can look bravely ahead, trusting the future into God's hands.

My Other Name Is Mom

CHAPTER NINETEEN

Happy Homemaking

Life would be less complicated if all we had to do was care for children. But being a stay-at-home mom involves a lot more than babysitting. While we're nursing babies, changing diapers, reading stories, wiping little noses, and putting first-aid cream on scraped knees, we're also doing fifteen loads of laundry a week, serving twenty-one meals, and cleaning the house—or at least making an attempt to do so. Not to mention buying groceries, organizing closets, defrosting freezers, spending weeks on window-covering decisions, and trying to make the house look nice on a budget. It's a lot to manage.

As a very young mother I often wondered how I was supposed to make it all happen. With children, I could no longer keep my house in the condition I liked. Sometimes I felt stressed and depressed. I was often exhausted and felt like there were mountains of things I wasn't getting done. How could I know if I was doing enough? How could I possibly get any more done? I often wondered if other ladies had a better system for managing, if they felt as stressed about all that wasn't getting done as I did, or if they happily filled out organizers and watched their weeks happen beautifully according to plan. Sometimes I felt like I must be the only one feeling so far behind and wondering, *Which thing is most important today?*

I still have those feelings at times, though not with the intensity I did then. There is an extra-difficult stretch in the beginning when you have a few little ones who all need help and who can't help you much yet. Even though my oldest is just ten, things are already easier for me. I have several children old enough to take care of themselves; and finally, I have some real help around the house. They can tidy up, sweep floors, clean their own bedrooms, put away their own laundry, and wash dishes.

Now, I find that though I have more help, I have more work to do and more to manage in general. I was curious how other moms manage, so I decided to find out. I found nine ladies willing to answer some questions about homemaking. These moms range in age from mid-twenties through mid-fifties.

They have between two and nine children and all of them currently have some children at home. These ladies grew up in a variety of areas and church groups. And don't worry—I did not handpick ladies who are super-organized. I just asked a variety of ladies I know. I relied on some of the information they provided to write this chapter. (The survey results are at the end of this chapter.) If you are a young mom trying to figure out how to balance children and housework, this is to you, with love. I hope it's helpful.

Making it home
There is more to homemaking than simply managing a home. While making sure everything happens when and how it should, we also create an atmosphere. We can get very focused on our houses and making them what we want them to be or pining because they aren't what we wish they were. But a homemaker can do something for a home that no amount of paint and décor could ever do. We can make the home a comfortable, welcoming, happy place where our family and friends and strangers alike feel welcome. This aspect of homemaking gives

depth and meaning to the most mundane daily tasks. Our homes are not a place we're stuck in against our will. They are our own little domains where we love to be.

A homemaker: "A person, usually a woman, who cares for her own home and family by cleaning, cooking nutritious meals, doing laundry, running errands, caring for pets, working with a budget, organizing, *etc*. She is her own boss and enjoys the freedom of creating her own schedule. She does not have time to be lazy." [1] Being a homemaker is serious business. If we are getting out of bed at the last minute, with no idea of what we should be doing, and moving aimlessly around the house all day, we're going to be frustrated. We need to take our responsibility seriously and learn how to manage our homes.

Challenges to homemaking

Let's look at some challenges we may face.

Working alone. As a new bride, my first hurdle was realizing how long it took me to do everything alone. At home, I worked with my mother and three sisters. When preparing for Sunday guests, we made a list and divided it up; we could make a lot happen on a Saturday. After I had my own home, I couldn't divide my list with anyone. When the children began to come, the amount I could accomplish dropped even lower. I quickly learned that if I wanted to have guests, I would have to plan ahead and work at my list all week.

Children's messes. The ongoing struggle for me to accept is how quickly the house gets "trashed." Just yesterday, I came home after being gone for the morning. I looked around the house with satisfaction and thought how nice it looked when we weren't in it all day. But hours later, as we went to bed, I wondered sadly how the mess happened so fast. It was hard for me to leave it and go to bed. But this morning, I comfort myself that we had a happy evening and the children were occupied in constructive projects.

With five children and their toys and projects in a smallish house, the house seldom looks the way I want it to look for more than half an hour. One thing that helps me cope with the untidiness is to keep certain areas clean. It doesn't feel as overwhelming that way. One room I absolutely refuse to allow to get cluttered is our bedroom. That's one spot I can walk into and feel peaceful. And when I don't have time to straighten up the whole house right away, quickly cleaning the least untidy area can make me feel better.

Making meals. I always loved to cook. As a teenager, I was the primary cook in our home for a while, so I had lots of practice. As a newlywed, I was excited about buying my own groceries and cooking in my own kitchen. I thought I would never run out of creativity with food. A few short years later, I was tired of grocery shopping, and I often found myself wondering anxiously what to make for supper as the supper hour drew relentlessly nearer.

I still struggle with this sometimes, but I've learned it helps a lot to plan—if not a week ahead, at least the supper menu right after breakfast. One benefit of that is that I've started to use my slow cooker more. Nothing makes me feel more virtuous than having supper in a slow cooker. Some ladies make rotating meal schedules for weeks at a time. Others frequently come right up to suppertime wondering desperately what to have. We're all different. The same method probably wouldn't even work for all of us. The plan doesn't really matter: the goal is to try to avoid the late afternoon anxiety. Nobody needs that extra stress.

I was once chatting with a group of ladies, and the conversation devolved into complaints about coming up with meals all the time. One lady gently put it into perspective when she commented on how much worse it would be to have nothing to feed our families. When I consider how horrible it would be to watch my children starve, I don't feel like complaining anymore. Even if we are on a tight budget, we are much more well-fed than many people in the world.

Getting organized

I have often suspected everyone's life is more well-ordered than mine, but I'm not so sure anymore. Some women are more naturally organized. Some of us try to get organized every once in a while, just because we think we should. Some women love to use plan books to organize their weeks. I have talked with women who say they would be lost without a written schedule; it keeps them on track even if they don't get everything done. I carried a bit of subconscious guilt for years because I don't use one. I found it interesting that none of my survey participants are plan-book users. They make it happen anyway.

Personally, I rely heavily on lists, since I am overwhelmingly absentminded. I keep running grocery lists and lists of other things we need, categorizing them by the stores where I usually shop. I keep lists of big things I want to accomplish, like sewing or defrosting the freezers, and work them in on my least busy days of the week. I keep lists of books I want to read and clothing the children need.

Don't underestimate the value of a ten-minute job. Waiting for a large slot of time to tackle a big job gets discouraging, but ten minutes spent cleaning something that is bugging me makes me feel so much better. I have seen plans for cleaning your entire house by working at it just ten or twenty minutes a day. And I'll admit that a lot of my cleaning happens on an as-needed basis, and sometimes on a way-overdue basis. The effects have not been harmful to our health.

Managing the work

In order to be effective homemakers, we must take care of ourselves. Running ourselves ragged for our families is not managing well. We should not be slaves to the system. We each need to find the balance in what is enough and what is too much. We should also have a system for our children to help. They can learn responsibility while lightening our load. At first, it is more work to teach them how to do it right, but it pays off in a short time.

One older mother observed that some moms are more work-oriented and some are more child-oriented. Those who are more work-oriented are in more danger of neglecting their children and stressing out. Others may do better at spending time with their children but need more discipline to get their housework done. We each need to figure out where we fit on this spectrum and what we need to work on.

Here is a summary drawn from the survey: The wishes of our husbands and the needs of our children should take priority in our schedules. When it comes to housework, food is most important. That doesn't mean it needs to be fancy. It's not sensible to take time away from something else when that food will be inhaled within fifteen minutes anyway (though there are exceptions for special occasions). After food comes laundry. It's helpful to have specific laundry days and complete the task within that day if at all possible. These three things—family, food, and clothing—can push cleaning and organizing much farther down the list than we'd like. With little ones, we will not be able to keep up with everything as we had before. We have two choices: get outside help or lower our standards. We'll probably have to do both at the busiest seasons of our motherhood.

I will quote a wise tidbit from the survey: "What gets done in a day gets done; whatever doesn't will be there tomorrow. It just wastes energy stressing out over it."

Happy homemaking to all!

Homemaking Survey

What does the term *homemaker* mean to you?

- Someone who keeps the home running smoothly and makes it a comfortable place to be. Mother sets the tone for the home. Sing or hum. Express appreciation for any help we get. Be thankful for all the small gifts of life; express this thankfulness to our families.

- Creating an atmosphere that is the heart of a home and restores and rests all who enter.

- I am responsible for making the home run smoothly. To do the tasks around the house.

- Making my home welcoming and comfortable to my family and guests and making delicious and nutritious meals and snacks for them.

- Beneath all the hard work of being a homemaker there needs to be a cheerful, accepting spirit. The atmosphere of the home is largely up to the homemaker. Being perceptive of the needs of my husband and children and learning how to meet them. Not only keeping the family clothed, fed, and comfortable, but also caring about their spiritual life and being discerning about dangers.

- I tend to think of a woman who is privileged to take a house "shell" and by applying her heart, hands, and interest to the project, makes it a home where her husband and children enjoy being (and she likes to be there too).

• Staying at home to serve my husband's and the family's needs, keeping the home a comfortable and happy place ready to serve friends and strangers as well.

• Staying at home most of the time and doing the housework and cooking myself instead of hiring someone else to do it. And letting my home be used by God through having company, *etc.*

• A stay-at-home mom.

What aspect of homemaking do you find the most challenging?

• Maintenance: repainting, repairs, replacing worn things like furniture and curtains

• Balancing the urgent and the important

• The everyday work, doing it over and over

• Keeping the house tidy is probably the most challenging. Notice I didn't say spotless—I've pretty much given up on that. Probably spotless never was one of my aims. Planning meals would be a close second.

• Learning to have the same priorities as my husband. For example, my husband likes when I'm available to help him sometimes or go along with him just for the fun of it. Listen to what he wants and make that a priority and not what I think is most important.

• The parts I don't like, of course. For me cleaning is what gets pushed off until the dirt can't be ignored.

• Keeping ahead of the dirt

• Keeping bathrooms clean

• Keeping my house clean

What part of housekeeping was most unexpected?

- The joy and contentment found in being a homemaker.

- That I can't do it all.

- How mundane housework is.

- How quick everything went to rack and ruin after I cleaned!

- Being responsible for shopping. Managing money or a budget. How time-consuming the care of a baby is.

- I was unprepared for seeing aspects of myself that showed up when I was the only one doing everything. I had always thought it was "the rest of them" who didn't put their things away, and I had nine handy scapegoats to blame when something of my own had been mislaid... until I got married!

- Another meal to serve, very demanding job to provide good nutritious meals and on schedule

- How dirty bathrooms get

- Keeping my husband happy

What is your favorite household task?

- Washing dishes and laundry

- Cleaning and organizing

- Vacuuming floors

- Grocery shopping. (Especially if I have the funds to get everything I need. Or maybe I should say especially when I can get everything on my list without feeling guilty for how much I spent!)

- I enjoy outdoor work like gardening and yard work more than indoor work.

- There is really nothing I hate. But a shining clean oven gives me a sense of satisfaction and I love the Saturday night clean-house-(almost!)-everywhere look.
- Cooking and laundry
- Laundry
- Laundry and hanging it outside on the wash line to dry, it has a fresh smell

Share a housekeeping tip you've learned.

- Have a place for everything and put things away as soon as you're finished with them.
- One of the things that helps me get things done is to have certain chores for certain days (besides a day's everyday chores, like dishes) and not get distracted till that chore is finished.
- If you keep up the housework every day, it helps not to feel overwhelmed.
- Bleach is an economical toilet bowl cleaner, rubbing alcohol works wonders on faucets. When you're in a hurry, salad mixes from Wal-Mart are just as cheap as buying the lettuce, red cabbage, and carrots separately, and much less time-consuming than shredding them all yourself.
- Instead of scolding the children when they make a mess, like spills, tracking mud, or breaking something, simply tell them to clean it up. They often already felt bad about it and were glad to try to make it right.
- PUT THINGS AWAY! You can't train your husband to do this—I mean you shouldn't—and your children might take after him in not putting their books back on the shelf, their shoes in the closet, and worse, but you can make a difference yourself. Resolve not to walk through your house empty-handed; pick up SOME-

THING that is out of place as you go past it and put it back where it belongs.

• I hate clutter when I come back from shopping or being away. We empty out the van and all items get placed on a designated pile. Each bedroom has a clutter-collecting spot. Then the children and I can quickly grab things to put in proper closets or drawers.

• Stressing out about what didn't get done makes you (and your family) unhappy. You won't rest well, and therefore you won't have the energy to complete the task. Just do your best and leave the rest.

• Getting rid of the clutter helps to keep your sanity.

Do you use a plan book/organizer to schedule your work?

• No. I've found it helps to fill one out, but I never stick with it exactly. Just the fact of writing things down helps me organize my work.

• No. I don't use a written schedule.

• Some weeks; working on perfecting my schedule.

• No. I don't use a plan book or organizer. They are too intimidating and time-consuming for me.

• No. I planned ahead which days to get certain things done. Most times my work is flexible.

• No. I object to the clutter they make on my counter. I will sometimes scribble an upcoming event on the calendar or write a reminder to myself and put it on the refrigerator, but that's all.

• All important projects/appointments are written on the calendar.

• No

• No

Do you use lists?

• When getting company or feeling overwhelmed.

• The only list I make is a grocery list.

• Not a lot

• The only times I use lists are before we leave on a trip or when I'm getting ready for company.

• I mostly use grocery lists. Occasionally I make a job list.

• I do—sometimes more detailed than others. As the girls were growing up, it seemed to help all of us stay on track to know what the goals were if I posted the jobs that needed to happen. I tend to keep both a long-term and a short-term list going, and it's a feeling of accomplishment to strike off the time-consuming larger projects on the first, while the second keeps me focused on the urgencies of the day. If I try to get along without a written plan, I fritter away a lot of golden moments, I have learned.

• I write "must dos" on a daily list, then write possibilities on the bottom of the tablet in case I have time during the week. I try to keep plenty of space for numerous important family needs, or I may need to go to town for shop supplies when my husband needs more paint.

• Occasionally

• Yes, when very busy

Other methods of managing:

• Have children help, even if they don't do things perfectly. Don't be afraid to ask company to help with bringing food. Only clean where it's necessary, not just because it's cleaning day again. Don't have too many things.

• Making it a regular habit to tidy the whole house as a family two or three times a day keeps things much more manageable.

• I have a magnetic whiteboard on my fridge if I'm having a particularly busy week and I don't want anything to fall through the cracks. Otherwise, what gets done in a day gets done and whatever doesn't will be there tomorrow. It just wastes energy stressing out over it.

• When time is pressing, my mom said having food is more important than cleaning. When one of the children was sick and I felt overwhelmed because I wasn't reaching around, my husband used to tell me caring for the child's needs comes first. Learn to live with my limitations. An overworked homemaker with overstrained nerves who becomes impatient or makes unreasonable demands is not managing well.

• Writing a collection of food ideas down, especially when I have plenty of a certain kind of food needing to be used up, makes meal planning faster. Try keeping laundry days to twice a week and put it all away before night. One day for weekly cleaning, then I can focus on other projects all week, knowing those jobs will get done.

• I have specific days for specific jobs.

• Let my husband do the managing sometimes. It may not be the way I would do it, but at least it gives him a taste of what I do as a wife.

Name one thing you've decided is not important.

• Having things perfect. We do have to keep working at being a homemaker, but we don't want to be a slave to housework.

• Doing weekly cleaning all in one day.

- To have a clean house is not important, but to have my family feel loved and important is.

- One thing that isn't important to me is spring and fall housecleaning.

- What other people think.

- It used to matter a lot to me what other people might think of how I kept—or didn't keep—house. Now it doesn't bother me. I try to stay current on things that are important to my husband first of all, consider my family's preferences next, and the other people can think what they want to. I don't live with them, after all.

- Keeping my home spotless. I now try to keep it clean enough to be comfortable, but dirty enough to have a happy family instead of an uptight mom!

- A fancy meal for company

- A spotless clean house

What makes you feel happy about your home?

- I'm happy about my homemaking when my family is happy to be here.

- Our home is our family's favorite place to be and guests comment on finding it relaxing and peaceful.

- That we can be ourselves here.

- One thing that makes me happy about my home is that it's "clean enough to be healthy and dirty enough to be happy."

- Faith that God can take the little I do and bless it if I'm yielded to Him. "Little is much if God is in it; Man's busiest days are not worth God's minute; Much is little everywhere, if God the labor does not share. So work for Him and nothing's lost. Work on, work on! Who works with Him does most and best; work on, work on." (Author unknown)

- Christian husband and children chatting happily around a good meal, clean clothes in the drawers, able to open my home to friends and strangers anytime because I feel comfortable with what God has blessed us with.
- Clean floors and company
- My family—it's a blessing.

My Other Name Is Mom

Notes

Chapter One: Created to Nurture
1. Sarrah Le Marquand: It should be illegal to be a stay-at-home mum. March 20, 2017. The Daily Telegraph .https://www.dailytelegraph.com.au/ rendezview/sarrah-le-marquand-it-should-be-illegal-to-be-a-stayathome-mum/news-story/fbd6fe7b79e8b4136d49 d991b6a1f41c. February 27, 2018.
2. Marquand: It should be illegal to be a stay-at-home mum. March 20, 2017. The Daily Telegraph.
3. Modern Parenthood: Roles of Moms and Dads Converge as They Balance Work and Family. March 14, 2013. Pew Research Center. https://www.pewsocialtrends.org/2013/03/14/modern-parenthood-roles-of-moms-and-dads-converge-as-they-balance-work-and-family/. February 27, 2018.

Chapter Three: A Case for Babies
1. Nicholas Bakalar. U. S. Fertility Rate Reaches a Record Low. July 3, 2017. The New York Times. https://www.nytimes.com/2017/07/03/health/united-states-fertility-rate.html. March 1, 2018.
2. The Changing Child Population of the United States. An Analysis of the U.S. Population Under 18 Using Data From the 2010 Census. The Annie E. Casey Foundation. www.aecf.org/resources/ the-changing-child-population-of-the-united-states/. March 1, 2018.
3. Tomas Frejka. December 11, 2017. Half the World's Population is Reaching Below Replacement Fertility. Institute for Family Studies.

    https://ifstudies.org/blog/half-the-worlds-population-is-reaching-below-replacement-fertility. March 1, 2018.
4. Anne Taylor Fleming. Motherhood Deferred: A Woman's Journey. Page 19
5. Sky Dylan-Robbins. November 24, 2014. Egg Freezing: A Hope, Not a Promise. The New Yorker. https://www.newyorker.com/tech/ elements/egg-freezing-hope-promise. March 15, 2018.
6. Ariana Eunjung Cha. January 27, 2018. She championed the idea that freezing your eggs would free your career. But things didn't quite work out. https://www.washingtonpost.com/ classic-apps/brigette-adams-became-the-poster-child-for-freezing-your-eggs-but-things-didnt-quite-work-out-how-she-imagined/2018/ 01/27//ff55857a-e667-11e7-833f-155031558ff4 story.html?utm term=. eda3cc95f904. March 15, 2018.

Chapter Four: Feminism and Me

1. Jan Marsh. 'The Personal is Political': Gender in Private & Public Life in the 19th Century. http://www.vam.ac.uk/content/articles/p/the-personal-is-political-gender-in-private-and-public-life/. April 24, 2019.
2. Women in the EU: Women in the History of Europe. www.helsinki.fi/science/xantippa/wee/weetext/wee214.html. March 3, 2018.
3. Victorian Women: The Gender of Oppression. Historical Analysis: Women as "the Sex" During the Victorian Era. http://webpage.pace.edu/nreagin/tempmotherhood/fall 2003/3/hispage. html. April 23, 2019.
4. When did women begin wearing pants. Christin Conger. October 2, 2013. Stuff Mom Never Told You. https://www.stuffmomnevertoldyou.com/ blogs/when-did-women-begin-wearing-pants. html. March 3. 2018.
5. W. Bradford Wilcox. Fall 2009. The Evolution of Divorce. National Affairs. March 22, 2019. https://www.nationalaffairs.com/publications/ details/the-evolution-of-divorce.

Notes

6. Urban Dictionar. https://www.urbandictionary. com/define.php?term=Third%20Gender. March 2018
7. David Lucciano Thompson. Third Wave Feminism. April 5, 2016. Odyssey https://www. theodysseyonline.com/third-wave-feminism March, 2018

Chapter Five: Feminism at Home

1. *Walt Larimore, MD and Barb Larimore*. His Brain, Her Brain: How Divinely Designed Differences Can Strengthen Your Marriage. Pages *30-37*.
2. Leon J. Podles. *The Church Impotent: The Feminization of Christianity*. Chapter 2: "Can a Man Be a Christian?"
3. Feminine Christianity turns men away from church, CBMW Executive Director says. April 18, 2006. https://cbmw.org/uncategorized/ feminine-christianity-turns-men-away-from-church-cbmw-executive-director-says/ April 25, 2019
4. *Leon J. Podles*. The Church Impotent: The Feminization of Christianity. Page *208*.

Chapter Six: Equality in the Kitchen

1. *Anne Taylor Fleming*. Motherhood Deferred: A Woman's Journey. *Page 175*
2. *Joe Tanenbaum*. Male & Female Realities. Understanding the Opposite Sex. *Pages 87 & 88*

Chapter Eight: What About a Social Life?

1. Patti Neighmond. April 21, 2014. For the Children's Sake, Put Down That Smartphone. Shots-Health New From NPR. https://www.npr.org/ sections/health-shots/2014/04/21/304196338/for-the-childrens-sake-put-down-that-smartphone November 15, 2017.

Chapter Fourteen: Enjoying the Little Years

1. Joyce Witmer. Excerpt from letter. April 2018

Chapter Fifteen: The Needs of Little Ones

1. At What Age is the Brain Fully Developed? Mental Health Daily. https://mentalhealth

135

daily.com/2015/02/18/at-what-age-is-the-brain-fully-developed/ March 20, 2018

Chapter Sixteen: Our Children's Happiness

1. Needham Public Schools. Child Labor in Factories During the Industrial Revolution. https://www2.needham.k12.ma.us/nhs/cur/Baker_00/2002_p7/ak_p7/childlabor.html February 20, 2018
2. Alan Taylor. Child Labor in America 100 Years Ago. The Atlantic. July 1, 2015. https://www.theatlantic.com/photo/2015/07/childlabor-in-america-100-years-ago/397478/ February 20, 2018.

Chapter Eighteen: Looking into the Future

1. E. Prentiss. *Stepping Heavenward*. Page 241

Chapter Nineteen: Happy Homemaking

1. Urban Dictionary. https://www.urbandictionary.com/define.php?term=Homemaker.

Acknowledgements

I couldn't have written this book without the input of others. I appreciate everyone who was interested and supportive. A special thank you to those who took time to offer advice and to help me make my thoughts coherent.

Thank you:

- To my husband, Lyndon, for encouraging and supporting me all the way. I value the mind-shaping conversations we have about everything. I don't know how best to credit your contribution because I'm not always sure where my thoughts stop and yours begin.
- To my editor, Jennifer Perfect, for helping me say it my way, only better. I loved working with you.
- To my mom, Christine Diller, for support and encouragement. As the first reviewer of the manuscript, you encouraged me enough that I sent it to others.
- To my sister, Analise Miller, for taking time out from chasing three little boys to critique the manuscript. I appreciated your honest criticism and generous praise.

- To my good friend, Sheila Nolt, for using precious downtime to let me know what resonated with her and what didn't. I really appreciate the conversations that jump-started my mind when I was stuck on how to wrap up an idea.
- To Stephanie J. Leinbach, for valuable feedback. You told me what was wrong with my early manuscript in a way that assured me there was some good in it.
- To Titania Porter, for final scrutiny and fine-tuning. I appreciated your valuable suggestions.
- To Joyce Witmer, for ample affirmation and enthusiasm. You make being a mom of teenagers look fun.
- To Edwin Eby, for generous praise, kind criticism, and theological critique.
- To Vernon Martin, for doctrinal review.
- To the ladies who participated in the homemaking survey. Thank you for your time and openness.
- To all whom I have quoted: thank you. I value the conversations that helped shape this book.
- And finally, if you are one of the people who kept asking how this book was coming, a special thank you. You helped me stay focused and productive.